WHAT THE BIBLE TEACHES ABOUT
D E A T H

This series of books sets out to present what the Bible actually teaches. We have in mind a readership made up of people of all ages who are comparatively new to the Christian faith or who are feeling their way towards it.

Inevitably, some of the topics considered may be easier to deal with than others. All those who have contributed to the series have in some way or other been involved in a teaching ministry, but in presenting this series of books we are not writing primarily for theological students. Our concern is to help people who are enquiring about the Christian faith and those who have come to believe but who have not had a Christian background. In recent years there has been a tendency to regard Christian doctrine lightly, and to emphasize Christian experience and Christian living. What is needed is a balance between the various aspects of the Christian faith, so that both our experience and our way of life may be measured against the yardstick of what the Bible teaches.

We therefore present this series in the prayerful hope that some seekers after truth may come through to a living faith, and that those whose experience of Christ is new may be built up to become mature men and women of God.

While each book stands on its own feet, we recommend that those who desire to gain a full-orbed picture of what Christianity is all about should study the series as a whole.

EDITOR

WHAT THE BIBLE TEACHES ABOUT

DEATH

Peter Cotterell

SERIES EDITOR: G. W. KIRBY

Tyndale House Publishers, Inc. Wheaton, Illinois

Unless otherwise stated, Bible quotations are from the Revised Standard Version of the Bible.

Quotations from the New English Bible, second edition © 1970, are reproduced by kind permission of Oxford and Cambridge University Presses.

Library of Congress Catalog Card Number 80-80182. ISBN 0-8423-7887-1, paper. Copyright © 1979 by Peter Cotterell. First published in Great Britain, under the title *I Want to Know What the Bible Says about Death*, by Kingsway Publications, Ltd. Tyndale House edition published by arrangement with Kingsway Publications, Ltd. All rights reserved. First Tyndale House printing, July 1980. Printed in the United States of America.

CONTENTS

Night slipped to dawn and pain merged into beauty,
Bright grew the road his faithful feet had trod;
He gave his salutation to the morning
And found himself before the throne of God.

'The last enemy to be destroyed is death.'
1 Corinthians 15:26

INTRODUCTION

What is death? The biblical answer to this question is blunt: 'The wages of sin is death' (Romans 6:23). 'Sin pays a wage, and the wage is death' (New English Bible). Dr Leslie Weather-head liked to call it 'a milestone on the road'. Medically speaking, death is the final ceasing of the bodily functions.

Death is the end of one stage of our journey and the beginning of the next. It marks the end of living on earth and the start of a very much fuller life in heaven. For some. Because death is much more than the simple parting of body and spirit: the Bible consistently treats death as the ultimate crisis, the crisis at which for all time, no, for all *eternity*, our destiny is fixed: with God in heaven or without him in hell.

Death does mean parting with the physical body. That may seem tough to young people, because for them the body is still strong, light, obedient. For those of us who are older, it's not so difficult to think of parting with the body, because it has gradually been getting more decrepit, more tattered through the years, and will no longer do all that we expect of it.

All that we expect of it! I'm not yet fifty, and yet my body won't do a fraction of the things I want it to do. My brain won't think straight, my eyes can't see straight, my legs won't walk far enough and my muscles won't work long enough. And perhaps it's because I'm aware of this weakening process that I'm not really so very much afraid of the thought of having to part with this body.

Death is the separation of the body and the spirit which gives it life. It's rather odd, in a way. The human body can be all there. Heart, veins, lungs, brain, everything in its place, and yet the body can be lifeless. It's much more than a marvellously intricate piece of machinery. It takes the breath of God to give it life. The book of Genesis is a great source book for the answers to almost all of the ultimate questions about people. In chapter 2 we find God making man:

... then the Lord God formed man of dust from the ground,

but that didn't produce life. The house was there, but there was no one living in it. The body was made but there was no *person* to give it life:

... and breathed into his nostrils the breath of life; and man became a living being (verse 7).

The breath of God creates life, and it is so every time new life is conceived by a woman. The woman forms the body, but God creates the spirit that gives life to the body.

Death comes to the body when the spirit leaves it, just as life comes to the body when the spirit enters it.

If we speak simply of physical death, death is the final ceasing of the bodily functions. The heart stops beating so that blood no longer circulates through the veins and arteries. The lungs no longer function so as to replenish the supply of oxygen in the blood. Perhaps most important of all, the brain stops functioning, and no longer sends out those impulses to the fingers to touch and the legs to bend, and the eyes to open, which constitute bodily life.

In the past it has been relatively easy to know when a person has died. Death was usually expected, and easily recognized; but now it is possible to provide a temporary heart to keep blood circulating, and temporary lungs to replenish the oxygen supply. So the person keeps breathing and his heart keeps beating in spite of the fact that if his artificial life supports were removed all of these activities would stop: he would be dead.

However, so far we have been unable to provide all the functions of the brain, so death today tends to be defined in terms of the non-functioning of the brain more than in terms of not breathing or no heart beat. With an electro-encephalogram it is possible to monitor the activity of the brain, and actually to show the pulses of energy produced by the brain, on a screen rather like a television. And when the brain stops its activity then the screen shows a flat line instead of the wavy line which is characteristic of the living brain. If that flat line trace continues then it is an indication that there is no brain activity at all and that the person is clinically dead. That's the doctor's concept of death.

Death may be the result of an accident, but most of us die simply as a result of the gradual deterioration of our bodies. They wear out, and although the doctors are able to make a good many temporary repairs, eventually the task gets beyond them. The body is like a tent (2 Corinthians 5:1) and like a tent it gradually wears out. The tent poles break, the canvas frays and the ropes snap. Until one day the tent blows down. That's death.

But from the point of view of what the Bible says, death is something very different. Death isn't just physical, not just an accident that can be avoided. It's not just an aging process that will one day be evaded by some kind of permanent bodily-spare-parts bank. Death is theological. It has to do with our relationship to God.

Because although we take death for granted, why *should* we die? There are some flowers that you can plant and they'll come up again, year after year. They seem to have solved the problem of eternal life all right. And even the humble amoeba has managed it. He may be well down in the scale of life, but in essence he lives for ever. Even the lobster can grow a new claw for himself. So why can't we hope to cheat death, to find a way of generating new limbs to replace those lost in some accident? Why not find a way of sleeping through the dark winters, to emerge in fresh life each spring? Why not study the amoeba and learn to live for ever? The answer is theological:

It is appointed for men to die once, and after that comes judgement (Hebrews 9:27).

These words mean more than that death is a kind of cosmic accident that eventually takes us all. No, 'it is *appointed*', death is on the agenda, literally 'in the store'. It is on the agenda for historical reasons. As Paul expresses it: '... sin came into the world through one man' (Romans 5:12).

Death as we know it today is an intrusion. It is not what God had planned for us. The sin of the first man, his disobedience to a simple prohibition, his willingness to doubt what God had told him, these things brought death, as we know it, into the world. Death is the wage earned by sin.

1
SOME BIBLICAL THEMES

Would Adam have died if he had not sinned?

He certainly would not have died in the way that he *did* eventually die. And certainly Abel would not have died as *he* died, murdered by his brother, if Adam had not sinned. Death as we now know it, with its fears and hurts and mysteries — that kind of death would not have existed.

I think that I would be quite ready to think of life on this earth coming to an end for Adam, for his successors, even if Adam had not sinned. I suppose that in *that* sense Adam might have 'died', might have been transferred from this world to heaven. In the first chapter of Genesis, God creates man and woman and then tells them:

Be fruitful and multiply, and fill the earth ... (verse 28).

Had there been no 'death' the world must inevitably have become uncomfortably crowded! Just *how* God might have taken people off to glory, of course, we don't know. Maybe like Enoch, who appears to have absentmindedly gone walking and talking with God and got so wrapped up in it that he blundered on into heaven; or maybe like Elijah who was swept up to heaven in a fiery chariot.

If I'm allowed to add my own comment here, I would expect that Adam would have gone to glory rather in the same way as Christians will get to glory if they are still alive here when Christ returns. According to 1 Thessalonians 4:17, when Christ returns the Christians who are still alive will be caught up to meet Christ in the air, and so they will be for ever with the

Lord. Obviously their bodies will have to be changed to match the resurrected bodies of Christians who die before Christ's return. I would suggest that Christ's work at Calvary reversed the work of the disobedient first man, and that amongst those things reversed was this matter of death. And that although death is changed for Christians *now*, his return in glory will see the final reversal of the catastrophic change brought about by Adam's sin, the end of death as we know it, and the restoration of God's original intention: a glorious, peaceful transformation from this world to heaven. But of course I don't *know* that.

Why is dying sometimes referred to as 'crossing Jordan'?

I remember that great American preacher Dr Donald J. Barnhouse warning us never to take our theology from the hymn book. Hymns may provide good poetry, but they often provide bad theology. The metre of the *hymn* may be going *ta-ta-ta, pause, ta-ta-ta, pause*, while the theology wants to go *ta-tiddley tump, ta-tiddley tump*. And the two just won't agree. But since the hymn writer is dealing with poetry, the theology may have to give way to the requirements of poetry. And that's how the river Jordan gets into theology as a picture of death.

Of course, John Bunyan didn't help. Mr Valiant-for-truth is summoned to heaven, and has to cross the river to get there:

> Then said he, 'I am going to my father's; and though with great difficulty I am got hither, yet now I do not repent me of all the trouble I have been at to arrive where I am. My sword I give to him that shall succeed me in my pilgrimage, and my courage and skill to him that can get it. My marks and scars I carry with me, to be a witness for me that I have fought his battles who will now be my rewarder.'
>
> When the day that he must go hence was come, many accompanied him to the river side, into which, as he went, he said, 'Death where is thy sting?' And as he went down deeper he said, 'Grave, where is thy victory?' So he passed over, and all the trumpets sounded for him on the other side.

William Williams, the writer of the great hymn *Guide me, O Thou Great Jehovah*, is quite obviously carried away by the many very real parallels between the life of the Christian and the history of the Jews in their escape from Egypt. He looks at the guidance through the desert, the manna from heaven which fed God's people, the water struck from the rock, and then the crossing of the river Jordan:

> When I tread the verge of Jordan
> bid my anxious fears subside;
> Death of death, and hell's destruction,
> land me safe on Canaan's side:
> Songs of praises
> I will ever give to Thee.

But it must be admitted that Canaan, when looked at through the pages of the Bible, makes a very poor picture of heaven, with its battles and defeats! It has its victories too, and there could have been more victories had there been more faith. And that makes the crossing of Jordan much more a matter of *sanctification* than of death.

But the Bible does at least hint to us that our fears can be pictured in terms of crossing a river. Isaiah 43:2 expresses a great promise:

> When you pass through the waters I will be with you;
> and through the rivers, they shall not overwhelm you.

However, Isaiah is not actually referring directly to death. His reference to waters and the flooding rivers must be taken together with the following reference to the danger of fire. Isaiah is simply assuring Israel that come flood or fire God will always be there to see them through. And yet the Bible recognizes that death *is* an enemy ('The last enemy to be destroyed is death', 1 Corinthians 15:26) and that we do, in some measure, fear death. So that the imagery of a river to be crossed is a valid one.

Of course, William Williams wasn't the only hymn writer to use a river as an illustration of death; Charles Wesley did it too:

One family we dwell in Him,
One church above, beneath,
Though now divided by the stream,
The narrow stream of death....

So did Ray Palmer, in the chilling final verse of *My faith looks up to Thee*:

When ends life's transient dream,
When death's cold sullen stream
Shall o'er me roll;
Blest Saviour, then, in love,
Fear and distrust remove;
O bear me safe above,
A ransomed soul.

If it seems natural to use the idea of a river to picture the idea of death it is because the river has a *this* side and a *that* side. It represents an obstacle which must be passed. William Williams was a Methodist; he grew up in the countryside of Wales and later spent much of his time tramping the Welsh hills, preaching. Doubtless he crossed many a river and took many a drenching doing so. In his book *The Gospel in Hymns* A. E. Bailey suggests that Williams' Calvinism left him in uncertainty regarding his salvation, so that the 'anxious fears' were very real to him: was he saved or was he not?

It seems that it was this very real uncertainty that has conjured up for him and for many others the picture of death produced by river Jordan theology. Death is a frightening experience, it seems to say. The sullen waters, how cold they are. They are deep, too. Treacherous. *Will* we, in fact, ever get to the other side? I can understand why someone who is not a Christian should feel like that about the prospect of dying, but surely it ought not to be so for the man or woman who is committed to Christ.

What is 'the valley of the shadow of death' in Psalm 23?

Psalm 23 is the psalm of the good shepherd, but it is presented to us as the psalm of the sheep: 'The Lord is *my* shepherd.' It is fascinating to see how the psalm develops the story, as though taking us through a typical day in the life of the flock. The sheep comments on the shepherd who gives time, leisure, to enable the sheep to lie down in the green fields. The shepherd leads the sheep by still pools of water: not the raging hillside torrents, that can be so dangerous to the sheep, but the still, quiet, pools. And when the sheep does feel completely exhausted it is the shepherd who nurses it back to life again: 'he restores my soul,' he brings life back again.

And the shepherd leads his sheep. Along the pathway the shepherd walks ahead, a guarantee always that the path being taken by the sheep is the *right* path. For one thing this is for the safety of the sheep. For another thing the character, the good of the shepherd, depends on it being the right path: 'He leads me in paths of righteousness, in the right paths, for his name's sake.'

But not all of the experiences of the sheep are enjoyable ones. He walks by the side of the still pools and lies in green fields, but he sometimes walks in the valleys. We have to imagine the craggy rifts of the Judean hills. The sides of the valleys are steep, the valleys themselves are deep, and as the sun begins to set there are long dark shadows. It's not merely the darkness that the sheep fear: lurking in the shadows is the wolf, the mountain lion. But since the shepherd is there the sheep has no need to be afraid, even in the dark shadows.

Bible scholars have argued a great deal about the two words used in verse 4, 'shadow' and 'death'. Some scholars think that the two words mean just what they say, the shadow of death. Others interpret them rather differently as being simply a poetic way of talking about *total* darkness. Of course no Hebrew would be able to read those two words, whatever they might mean literally, without seeing there the idea of death: deep darkness, the very essence of death to the Jewish mind of David's day. The Jewish concept of death involved a shadowy land, a land of shades, a land of mystery. No one really knew what lay beyond the grave except that *something* most certainly did. So the metaphor of deep shadows and danger went well with the concept of death. And that's how most translators have taken the words: the valley of the shadow of death.

Towards the end of life we find ourselves having to give up the life of the mountain tops and the sunshine for the life of the shadows. As Churchill said of King George VI:

> During these last months the king walked with death, as if death were a companion, an acquaintance whom he recognized and did not fear.

We tend to face crises of health more frequently and from time to time we have to walk through the valley of the shadow of death itself. And then we are perplexed about this whole business of dying. This side of the gateway it's light enough, and Christians know it's all glory on the other side. But the gateway itself is dark. David was able to say, 'Even if I walk there I'll not be afraid of any evil, because you are with me.' I'll not be lost, I can't be robbed. We walk through the valley of the shadow of death and we come out of it safely, because the Shepherd is there with us.

Spurgeon commented on this verse:

> Often the last days of the Christian are the most peaceful in his whole career; ... many a saint has reaped more joy and knowledge when he comes to die than he ever knew while he lived.

When the Christian comes towards the end of his time here his days ought not to be clouded over by fears of the shadowy places surrounding this matter of dying. When we come to *that* the Shepherd will be right there.

Doesn't the Bible liken death to sleep?

All through history death has universally been looked upon as a calamity, as something bad, and usually as something not to be talked about. And so all languages seem to have developed euphemistic ways of talking about death. A euphemism is a gentle way of referring to a subject which might otherwise be unpleasant. Instead of talking about someone *dying*, we say that he has 'passed away', 'been called home', 'gone to his eternal rest', 'passed on' or even 'fallen asleep'.

We find that people in the Bible shared in this general reluctance to mention death. When Paul wrote his last letter, the second letter to Timothy, he was expecting execution at any time. But he could not quite bring himself to say just that. Or possibly he really had got hold of the truth about death and knew that death wasn't what it was generally supposed to be. Perhaps he knew that it was a beginning, not an ending. At all events he did not write to Timothy, 'I am about to die,' but he wrote, 'the time of my departure is at hand' (2 Timothy 4:6, Authorized Version).

In the Old Testament we find that when the kings died the historian recorded the fact that they 'slept with their fathers' (e.g. 2 Kings 8:24).

We can be quite sure that 'falling asleep' was a euphemism for death because of the conversation between Christ and his followers when Lazarus died. Mary and Martha sent messengers to tell Jesus that Lazarus was ill. In fact, by the time that the messengers reached Jesus, Lazarus was already dead, and Jesus knew it. But when he told them, he used the usual euphemism:

Our friend Lazarus has fallen asleep,
but I go to awake him out of sleep.

And the others misunderstood him:

Lord, if he has fallen asleep he will recover.

To make the point clear, the account goes on:

Now Jesus had spoken of his death, but they thought he meant taking rest in sleep. Then Jesus told them plainly, 'Lazarus is dead' (John 11:11–14).

The word 'sleep' is a euphemism for 'death'.

Obviously the word 'sleep' is a suitable alternative for the word 'death'. The person who is asleep lies still and does not answer if he is spoken to: there is an outward similarity. But we must be careful not to take this euphemism too far. Because there is one very great and extremely important difference between sleep and death. In sleep the person is still there, waiting to be awakened. In death the person is not there. The body may be physically all there, but it is already beginning the process of disintegration.

In fact, the Bible does *not* teach that at death the Christian falls asleep, and remains asleep until the day of judgement. The pious R.I.P., may he rest in peace, is a pious inscription and that is all. He, or she, is not resting under the pile of earth at all. The Bible teaches that the Christian leaves this life and at once goes to be with Christ ... 'absent from the body, and ... present with the Lord' (2 Corinthians 5:8, Authorized Version). When Christ returns to earth he will bring with him those who have been with him:

> For since we believe that Jesus died and rose again, even so, through Jesus, God will bring with him those who have fallen asleep (1 Thessalonians 4:14).

When Christ comes back he will bring with him all those Christians who have died, 'fallen asleep', and who, ever since they 'fell asleep', have been with Jesus.

The idea of 'falling asleep' is a very beautiful one because it is a reminder that the Christian has as much to fear from dying as he has to fear from falling asleep. Paul commented, 'The sting of death is sin' (1 Corinthians 15:56) and since for us sin has been dealt with by Christ, death has lost its sting.

Now you can skip this next section if you like, but somewhere I simply have to include a discussion of time and eternity. So this is it.

Once we die, time comes to an end. Time has to do with this world. We tell the time by a clock or a watch; we can tell the time by the rising of the sun; we can tell the season by the changing climate. We learn that there are sixty seconds in a minute and sixty minutes in an hour and twenty-four hours in a day. That's a convenient way of handling time, although a rather arbitrary way.

I say that it's arbitrary, because most of us know that time isn't in fact quite as regular as it is made out to be. Five minutes in a dentist's chair may seem like a couple of hours. A week's holiday can be gone as though it were no more than a day. But still, time is real enough: there was yesterday, there is today and there will probably be tomorrow.

But once we leave this universe, time no longer exists. The sun doesn't rise because there isn't any sun. But we find it almost impossible to think of existence at all, of any kind of life, which has no time in it. But we tend unthinkingly to transfer our patterns of thought and speech, suited to this world, over to the next world, where they are quite out of place. Tongue in cheek we talk about how dull it would be *after* the first century or two of eternity. Or we ask theological questions about what happens to a person *after* he has died but *before* Christ comes back. Or we wonder how a husband and wife will know one another again in heaven *after* they have been separated for twenty years.

Those categories of *before* and *after* simply don't apply to the next life. I would guess that there's no such thing as age in heaven. That somehow there is an essential *me* that isn't a boy, or a young man, nor even an elderly man, but is just *me*. My own experience already tends to confirm this, because I don't feel any particular age. Right now I don't feel that I'm middle-aged, although undoubtedly by the calendar that's exactly what I am. I am living in a tent which has an easily determined age. But that doesn't particularly seem to relate to *me*. This *me* is somehow independent of time. Now it's this real *me* that is set free from the body at death, and then 'marches into eternity'.

When I march into eternity I don't then have to 'wait' until eventually, one by one, my friends join me. Waiting is something that you measure by the clock and there are no clocks in glory.

So our loved ones are not 'waiting' over there, somehow getting older and wiser in spiritual mysteries and leaving us behind. We all get to heaven together, in eternity's everlasting now.

That's all a bit philosophical, maybe, but it may help us to realize that some of the questions we ask, and even some of the answers we give, have too much of this world about them, and too little of the next. But perhaps the philosophy will help us to get rid of some of our hang-ups about people in heaven waiting for the day of judgement, or waiting for loved ones to join them. The tyranny of time is smashed in the glory of eternity.

To return to our subject: death *is* called sleep in the Bible, and this is a euphemism. But we don't fall asleep at death: the Christian goes to glory. And we don't 'wait around' either for the judgement day, or for the coming to us of our loved ones: in glory there is no time. And the picture of sleep is a gentle reminder that we have as little to fear from death as we have from sleep. When Jesus laid down his life on the cross he spoke the prayer that Jewish children spoke each night as they went to sleep:

> Father, into thy hands I commit my spirit (Luke 23:46).

You couldn't find a better illustration.

What does 2 Corinthians 5:1 mean?

We'd better have the verse in question. Here it is, as it appears in the New International Version:

> Now we know that if the earthly tent we live in is destroyed, we have a building from God, an eternal house in heaven, not built by human hands.

This sentence by Paul is one of my favourites on the whole subject of dying, because the picture it presents is so simple and so very appropriate.

I was first made aware of the significance of the verse through a funeral service in Addis Ababa. A young Christian doctor,

Faith Rayner, had just died very suddenly. Actually she had just completed her tour of duty and was expecting to go home when she was taken ill, and suddenly she was gone. I shared in the funeral service, but a friend of mine preached. And I remember him saying something along these lines:

> Don't imagine that Faith is there, in that box. Oh no! The storm came and the wind blew, and the tent in which she had lived blew down. But Faith is all right. She moved out of the tent and into her home in heaven.

And immediately I could see it. Of course! That *is* how death comes. Often the tent has been showing signs of wear and tear for a good many years. The canvas frays, the ropes get thin, the tent pole cracks. The hair thins out, the teeth fall out, the hearing fails, the bones become ever more brittle, the joints creak. And then one day the wind blows just that little bit too hard, and down goes the tent. Ecclesiastes gives a magnificent word picture of the gradual onset of old age:

> Remember your Creator in the days of your youth, before the time of trouble comes and the years draw near when you will say, 'I have no pleasure in them.' Remember him before the sun and the light of day give place to darkness, before the moon and the stars grow dim, and the clouds return with the rain – when the guardians of the house tremble, and the strong men stoop, when the women grinding the meal cease work because they are few, and those who look through the windows look no longer [The Living Bible interprets: 'when your limbs will tremble with age, and your strong legs will become weak, and your teeth will be too few to do their work'], when the street doors are shut, when the noise of the mill is low, when the chirping of the sparrows grows faint and the song-birds fall silent; when men are afraid of a steep place and the street is full of terrors, when the blossom whitens on the almond tree and the locust's paunch is swollen and caper-buds have no more zest. For man goes to his everlasting home, and the mourners go about the streets. Remember him before the silver cord is snapped and the golden bowl is broken, before the pitcher is shattered at the spring, and the wheel broken at the well, before the dust returns to the earth as it began and the spirit returns to God who gave it (Ecclesiastes 12:1–7, New English Bible).

That's the kind of picture that lies behind 2 Corinthians 5:1. A house crumbling, the occupant looking out on to a world that means less and less to him.

But the deeper understanding of 2 Corinthians 5:1 depends on a whole sequence of thought that reaches back into chapter 3. The linking word is *glory*. The word occurs fifteen times from 3:7 to 5:1, usually referring to some marvellous indication of the presence of God. Paul's thoughts are back in the events of the Jews' Exodus from Egypt. Moses has been given the task of leading the Jewish people out of Egypt and into Canaan. But very early on in the journey he realizes that he can't cope with the task alone.

In Exodus 33 and 34 we find Moses talking with God. In the early part of chapter 33 Moses is seen going into the special *tent of meeting*, a kind of quiet place where anyone who wanted to pray could go and talk with the Lord. But when Moses went there himself it was different. As he began to walk towards that tent, we are told, the Israelites came out of their tents and stood in the entrance-ways to watch. It was always the same; as Moses went into the tent an unearthly cloud enveloped the doorway, and the cloud was the symbol that God was there, talking with Moses.

Moses wants to know: who is going to go with me on this journey? I can't make it alone:

> If thy presence will not go with me,
> do not carry us up from here.
> For how shall it be known that I have found favour in thy sight,
> I and thy people?
> Is it not in thy going with us?

Still Moses isn't satisfied. It's not enough that God promises to go with him: he must see God's glory. 'I need to know who you are ... I need to know your power. Can you cope? Show me ... show me your glory!' And in chapter 34 he sees it. Just a glimpse of it, but it is enough:

> And Moses made haste to bow his head towards the earth, and worshipped (Exodus 34:8).

Over the days which followed Moses went on communing with God, and as he did so his very face was transformed. Like the transfiguration in Luke 9, which took place on a different mountain, his face began to glow. But it was an outward reflection of an external experience. Moses' face reflected the glory of God which shone on him from outside.

Now in 2 Corinthians Paul is transferring Moses' unique experience into Christian experience. The Christian has a far greater privilege than Moses ever knew; with unveiled face we have the opportunity of meeting God each time we pray. With unveiled face, because Moses' face *was* veiled: he didn't understand all that was happening to him as having the deeper significance of salvation history. He didn't see the Exodus from Egypt as typifying the salvation of man from sin. It was so much of a mystery to him that he could only bow, and worship, but worship a mystery.

We understand a little more. For us the veil is removed inasmuch as we understand what happens is not merely external. We don't look at any outward display of God's glory, but experience it within. And it's not the outside that begins to glow, but the inside. Just as in the transfiguration the glory of Jesus broke through the concealing humanity of his body, shining *out*, and not merely reflecting something external, so in the life of the Christian an inner change, a transfiguration, is taking place, taking place continuously, changing his inner person, the real *me*, steadily, regularly, continuously, from one degree of glory to another.

But the process does take time. The years pass. And although the real, inward, nature is being transformed, renewed day by day, the outer, visible body is getting weaker. The diamond is gleaming ever more brightly, but the jewel case is getting battered: 'We have this treasure in earthen vessels' (2 Corinthians 4:7).

But, says Paul, we don't lose heart when we look at these aging bodies of ours, nor do we lose heart when we see other people involved in underhand practices and flourishing – materially – because of them. That's all on the outside. *Inside*, that's what really matters. The jewel inside the jewel case is being renewed, transformed, changed day after day, getting stronger, from one degree of glory to another, precisely as the body is getting weaker.

And Paul knew what he was talking about. He went through suffering: lashed by Jews and Romans, stoned, shipwrecked, tracked down, imprisoned; hungry, thirsty, tired (2 Corinthians 11:22-29). But he could accept all that because that side of it was temporary. His *was* a hard life, and it took a man like Paul, a man who had really suffered, to have the right to say just what he did say, to call suffering what he called it: 'this slight momentary affliction' (2 Corinthians 4:17). Of course he was right, but when we are in the midst of persecution and suffering it may not seem slight or momentary.

Suffering is of so many kinds. In the midst of it we can stand with Paul and see what he was getting at: life really is brief, in comparison with the weight of glory which is waiting up ahead. We can't always understand the tough things that hit us now, but we can hold on to the assurance that there is an answer up ahead. We do sometimes feel dog tired, and the body does drag when it just won't do all that we want it to.

But when the tent blows down, then we'll get the answers. Not another tent, but an eternal home prepared for us by Jesus: 'I go to prepare a place for you' (John 14:2). Here we offer him a place in our hearts. There he prepares a place for us, an eternal home. 'We do not lose heart.' Aching bodies and aching hearts. Tears and pains as well as laughter. And all the time our feet on the pathway to glory. Soon ... out of the tent and into glory.

How do you square Ecclesiastes 3:19 with the rest of the Bible's teaching about death?

Ecclesiastes 3:19 *is* a shock, when you first encounter it actually in the Bible. But the Bible says it, so we'd better be able to understand it. Here's what the verse says:

For the fate of the sons of men and the fate of beasts is the same; as one dies, so dies the other. They all have the same breath, and man has no advantage over the beasts; for all is vanity. All go to one place; all are from the dust, and all turn to dust again.

I suppose that the interpretation of this verse could be softened by pointing out that it actually refers primarily to death as the common experience of us all. People die, animals die. Our bodies turn to dust as do theirs. All end up in the grave. But this won't do as a total explanation of the verse, because this is just one of several verses all of which display a pessimism about life, and even more about death, which doesn't square with the rest of Scripture.

Let me bring together a few of these statements, all from Ecclesiastes.

What is crooked cannot be made straight, and what is lacking cannot be numbered (1:15).

There is nothing better for a man than that he should eat and drink, and find enjoyment in his toil (2:24).

Who knows whether the spirit of man goes upward and the spirit of the beast goes down to the earth? So I saw that there is nothing better than that a man should enjoy his work, for that is his lot; who can bring him to see what will be after him? (3:21–22).

Be not righteous overmuch, and do not make yourself overwise; why should you destroy yourself? Be not wicked overmuch, neither be a fool; why should you die before your time? (7:16–17).

... one fate comes to all, to the righteous and the wicked, to the good and the evil, to the clean and the unclean, to him who sacrifices and him who does not sacrifice. As is the good man, so is the sinner; and he who swears is as he who shuns an oath. This is an evil in all that is done under the sun, that one fate comes to all (9:2–3).

For the living know that they will die, but the dead know nothing, and they have no more reward; but the memory of them is lost (9:5).

Whatever your hand finds to do, do it with your might; for there is no work or thought or knowledge or wisdom in Sheol, to which you are going (9:10).

Again I saw that under the sun the race is not to the swift, nor the battle to the strong, nor bread to the wise, nor riches to the intelligent, nor favour to the men of skill; but time and chance happen to them all (9:11).

Now there's a great deal in there which directly contradicts the rest of Scripture: the blanket statement, 'the dead know nothing,' for example. As we understand it, time and *chance* do not happen to all: God has a *plan* which takes in everybody, including a heathen king Cyrus (Isaiah 44:28–45:5), and the King-Messiah whose sufferings were according to 'the definite plan and foreknowledge of God' (Acts 2:23). So how are we to understand Ecclesiastes?

The key to the understanding of the book is found in 1:13 –

I applied my mind to seek and to search out *by wisdom* all that is done under heaven.

Now the preacher, or teacher, presumably Solomon although he does not actually say so, was a man who had a very high view of his own wisdom:

I said to myself, 'I have acquired great wisdom, surpassing all who were over Jerusalem before me' (1:16).

It is on the basis of that wisdom that he sets out to understand and explain the mystery of life. Some three hundred years after Solomon, Gautama the Buddha set about the same task and almost a thousand years after that Muhammad tried again. These three, Solomon, Gautama and Muhammad were all setting about an impossible task. By ourselves we *cannot* understand God. Christianity does not present the results of man's quest for God, but it describes God's self-revelation to man.

But that's not the entire picture that I have given of the contents of Ecclesiastes. In point of fact the book of Ecclesiastes is a kind of dialogue, with Solomon, by wisdom alone, looking at life, and finding life completely pointless, and then with that same Solomon announcing that precisely since he can't make sense of life without God, man needs to behave in a certain way, recognizing God.

Notice the 'jam in the sandwich', the good things that are truly said about God, to counter the folly that Solomon speaks *as a man*:

> [God] has made everything beautiful in its time;
> also he has put eternity into man's mind,
> yet so that he cannot find out what God has done from the beginning
> to the end (3:11).

> I know that whatever God does endures for ever;
> nothing can be added to it,
> nor anything taken from it;
> God has made it so,
> in order that men should fear before him (3:14).

> I said in my heart, God will judge the righteous and the wicked,
> for he has appointed a time for every matter,
> and for every work (3:17).

> Be not rash with your mouth,
> nor let your heart be hasty to utter a word before God,
> for God is in heaven, and you upon earth;
> therefore let your words be few (5:2).

> Surely there is not a righteous man on earth who does good, and
> never sins (7:20).

> Rejoice, O young man, in your youth,
> and let your heart cheer you in the days of your youth;
> walk in the ways of your heart and the sight of your eyes.
> But know that for all these things
> God will bring you into judgement (11:9).

Ecclesiastes is an excellent book for the non-Christian. As he looks around him surely he must see just what *Koheleth*, the Preacher, saw. Man is born, a helpless child, struggles through youth and on into the years of carrying responsibility. He marries, has children, becomes old and then he dies, leaving his children to go through the same cycle again. And *their* children. Every generation passing inexorably away. Nor can any man know what his successor is going to be like. I build up a business with my toil and hard work and my knowledge. But I have little say as to who succeeds me in the business, and many a man has had a perfectly good business ruined by some incompetent successor.

The whole cycle of life and death does seem to be pointless. There is nothing really new to be done. True enough man goes to the moon, but before too long we find that it's not really so very different from landing on some lonely desert island. The spacecraft whirl above our heads and we can't be bothered any more to look up to spot the hurtling specks of light. Life is ridiculous.

Until we put God into it. And then we discover that this new dimension is the key to the entire picture. Leave God out ... despair. Put him in ... everything fits. If we have hope only in this life, said Paul, we are of all men most miserable. Well, that's just what makes the Preacher in Ecclesiastes miserable. He considers life as a closed system: just this world. And it is all vanity.

Ecclesiastes is a valuable reminder that it can be dangerous simply to quote off-handedly, 'the Bible says'!

What is baptism for the dead?

The idea of being 'baptized for the dead' appears in the Bible only in 1 Corinthians 15:29. In this section of Paul's letter he is dealing with the problem produced at Corinth by those who did not believe in the resurrection. Apparently some Corinthian Christians believed that death was the end. The only hope for the Christian was still to be alive when Christ returned. Paul uses several arguments against this point of view, and one argument stems from the practice of being baptized for the dead:

> Otherwise, what do people mean by being baptized on behalf of the dead? If the dead are not raised at all, why are people baptized on their behalf?

A number of explanations have been offered; I'll content myself with just three of the more plausible ones. The first two, it seems to me, are rather unlikely.

Firstly, then, there is the suggestion that for Paul the word *baptism* means baptism *into death* (Romans 6:3 – 'Do you not know that all of us who have been baptized into Christ Jesus were baptized into his death?'). So on this understanding of the text Paul is not speaking about water baptism but about *death*: some Christians, perhaps the first martyrs, were laying down their lives in order to be able to go to act as witnesses to the dead. We could then paraphrase 1 Corinthians 15:29 in the following way:

> Otherwise, what do the martyrs mean when they are immersed by the waters of death in order to be able to act as witnesses to the dead? If the dead are not raised then what sense is there in such a practice?

The objection to this interpretation is that while *baptism* does mean baptism into death, the death in mind is death to self, to the old nature, death with Christ at the cross, not physical death. Thus in Galatians 2:20,

> I have been crucified with Christ; it is no longer I who live, but Christ who lives in me,

and we note that in Romans 6:4 Paul goes on to explain the purpose of baptism into Christ's death as walking 'in newness of life'.

The second interpretation takes a different line. Instead of adding to the meaning of 'baptism', this view adds to the meaning of 'death'. The one who is being baptized is baptized as far as dead *works* are concerned. This suggestion has the advantage of being a possible rendering of the Greek and of being in line with Paul's teaching on the meaning of baptism. But, of course, the verse doesn't mention *works*, and the whole section of the letter is dealing with *death* and resurrection, not with dead *works*. But if this interpretation is accepted the verse becomes:

> Otherwise what do people mean when they are baptized so far as dead works are concerned?

We can get so far with this interpretation but no further. In the second part of the verse are we to use 'dead' as again meaning 'dead works', and if so what on earth does the sentence mean? Or are we to go back to the plain meaning 'death'; and if so why does the meaning of the word change in this way? Now this interpretation has a certain value to it: our *dying* to dead *works* (putting the two interpretations so far considered together) is ridiculous if, in fact, there is no resurrection and death ultimately ends everything. But while this further step makes better sense, it requires us to re-interpret *two* words in the passage instead of one.

Or we can take a third interpretation and alter no words at all. This does seem to be the most likely explanation of the verse. It would appear that at Corinth questions had been asked about the fate of those who were converted, but who died before being baptized. Now we know that very early on in the life of the church there developed a superstitious attitude towards baptism, so that it became almost magical in its power to deal with sin. Since there was so much else wrong with the theology of the church at Corinth I see no difficulty in expecting just such wrong-headedness to appear in relation to baptism.

Then what happened to these catechumens (as they might be called), new believers who, having believed and having been taught, died before being baptized? If baptism was essential to salvation, how could they receive baptism?

Two answers seem to have emerged. We know that a heretical group called the Marcionites, who flourished around A.D. 150, staged a kind of play for the dead person. The dead body was placed on a bed, and a friend of the dead person hid underneath the bed. Then an Elder would 'ask' the dead person if he wished to be baptized. The friend would then answer 'Yes!' and would himself be baptized in place of the dead person. This seems to be the more complicated, later development of a practice that existed at Corinth. There, a friend of the one who had died without being baptized was baptized instead. These two practices both seem to depend on the idea that salvation depends on being baptized.

What Paul is saying here is that since some Corinthian Christians were being baptized on behalf of their dead friends they must obviously believe in life after death, so that it was totally wrong for Bible teachers at Corinth to teach that there is no resurrection.

A word of caution needs to be added here. First of all, we don't *know* that this 'baptism on behalf of the dead' was being practised at Corinth, but this particular verse would certainly suggest it. Secondly we notice that Paul mentions the practice, but he does not commend it. He doesn't say, 'This is what you ought to do,' but he comments: 'This is what you are doing.' Thirdly we should note that Paul does *not* teach that we are saved by being baptized. The Bible teaches:

> by grace you have been saved (Ephesians 2:5);
> for by grace you have been saved through faith; and this is not your own doing, it is the gift of God (Ephesians 2:8);
> For there is no distinction; since all have sinned and fall short of the glory of God, they are justified by his grace as a gift, through the redemption which is in Christ Jesus (Romans 3:22–24).

Why didn't Adam die on the day he ate the forbidden fruit, as God had warned?

He did. Let's look at the wording of the original warning, and then at the condition of the entire human race. In Genesis 2 we have the account of the formation of man, and the planting of the garden of Eden. Man was placed there to care for it, and to enjoy it. All of it was at his disposal with the exception of one tree: the tree of the knowledge of good and evil:

> ... of the tree of the knowledge of good and evil you shall not eat, for in the day that you eat of it you shall die (Genesis 2:17).

It is very important to notice that *two* trees are marked out for special attention in this creation story: the tree of life and the tree of the knowledge of good and evil. The fruit of the tree of life was available to man but the fruit of the other tree was forbidden.

The temptation to man came as a questioning of what God had said. Adam was compelled to choose between what he had heard God say and what he was now being told: 'You will not die' (Genesis 3:4). He chose to ignore what God had said. Both man and woman ate and then:

> ... the eyes of both were opened, and *they knew* that they were naked; and they sewed fig leaves together and made themselves aprons (Genesis 3:7).

Notice that the fruit of the tree did give them knowledge, but nothing else of any great importance seemed to happen to them just then. It was a little later that God confronted them and they were expelled from their garden.

But I understand the Bible to teach that by then they were already actually spiritually dead. To be spiritually dead is the experience of every one of us until the grace of God brings us back to spiritual life again. The Bible teaches us that Adam brought a *double* death. Paul's words in 1 Corinthians 15:22 refer to ordinary, physical death:

> For as in Adam all die, so also in Christ shall all be made alive.

This is something still future. Paul is writing about the future resurrection.

Because Adam brought *physical* death of the kind that now awaits us all, there must be a resurrection from that physical death. But from the Bible we learn of another death that has already taken place:

> But God, who is rich in mercy, out of the great love with which he loved us, even when *we were dead* through our trespasses, made us alive together with Christ (Ephesians 2:5–5).

> And you he made alive, when *you were dead* through the trespasses and sins in which you once walked (Ephesians 2:1–2).

And *you, who were dead* in trespasses and the uncircumcision of your flesh, God made alive together with him (Colossians 2:13).

For the love of Christ controls us, because we are convinced that one has died for all; therefore *all have died* (2 Corinthians 5:14).

... yield yourselves to God as men who have been brought *from death* to life (Romans 6:13).

These passages of the Bible all agree that man is already spiritually dead. The Bible does not suggest that unless we become Christians we will die spiritually; it insists that until we are brought to life by Christ we *are* dead. This fully agrees with the experience that most of us have had when trying to talk with people who are not yet Christians. We feel that what we are saying is simple enough and quite obvious. But the other person doesn't seem to understand at all. So we may try to put it a different way, and still it is not clear.

I remember very well that when I was a young Christian a few of us arranged Sunday night meetings in an old tin hut, and we used to fish young people off the streets of the town where I lived and talk to them about God. One young fellow came in, and he was always full of questions. Every week I tried to answer one batch, but the next week he was ready with another batch. Eventually I became tired of this and I said to him:

'Malcolm, I believe that one day you are going to become a Christian and then you will wonder why ever you asked so many stupid questions!'

But Malcolm wasn't convinced:

'No, I can't become a Christian unless I get these questions answered.'

The very next Saturday, Malcolm went to hear Billy Graham and was converted. Turned right round. And on the Sunday he appeared in our tin hut as usual. So I asked him,

'Malcolm, how does it feel to be a Christian?'

He grinned:

'It's fine ... but I don't know why I asked so many stupid questions!'

The point was that all the while he was asking questions, Malcolm was spiritually dead. The answers didn't do him any harm but the questions kept him from making any commitment to God. He was *dead*. And then he was brought to life. The first Adam killed him. The last Adam brought him back to life.

It was this spiritual death that Adam died when he disobeyed God's command.

Incidentally it is very important to notice that just as we *were* dead, spiritually, before we became Christians, so now, if we *are* Christians we *have* eternal life:

Truly, truly, I say to you, he who believes *has* eternal life (John 6:47).

These two truths belong together. The Bible does not say that unless we believe we shall die: it says that the person who does not believe is dead. The Bible does not say that if we believe we will later on receive eternal life: it says that if we have believed then we already have eternal life. Eternal life, the life of eternity, is to begin here, and if you haven't got it before you die, you won't get it after you die.

2
COPING WITH DEATH

How can I explain death to my children?

Let me say straight away: you must be quite sure that you understand what the Bible says about death *yourself* before you try to explain it to children. Because children ask some very shrewd questions and they will at once know if you don't really have the right answers. And what's worse they can become seriously confused if you cannot answer clearly.

Very often the question asked by a child is not 'What is death?' but 'Why won't my dog talk to me now?' Other questions will follow: 'Why do we have to put him into the ground?' 'Why can't I keep him?' And so on. Sometimes the child may be distressed by the sight of an accident, or perhaps perplexed by the sight of a dead rabbit, just a mouldering pile in a field. Ultimately the whole question arises when a relative dies and the same questions are asked, but perhaps with greater urgency. It takes common sense, confidence, faith and knowledge of what the Bible has to say to us to answer these questions correctly. For if they are answered correctly the child can be immeasurably strengthened and enabled to understand what others may find an impenetrable mystery.

The subject of death is like the subject of sex in one way: if we are to be able to explain it helpfully we must not be embarrassed by it. Death, after all, is a natural part of life. It demands some explanation. In particular, the Christian ought to be able to explain it because Christianity has a whole theory about death and resurrection, and life and the life to come.

First of all, why do we not keep the body of the one who has died. The answer is because the human body is made out of the same materials as the things around us (Genesis 2:7) and when I leave my body it simply goes back into those materials again. It won't keep. 'Where has Auntie gone?' The question itself shows that children often know intuitively that Auntie *has* gone. The answer here will depend on the circumstances. If she was a Christian then the answer is plain: she has gone home to be with Jesus. If she was not known to be a Christian the answer must be more carefully worded. Because we don't *know* that she was not a Christian when she died. The answer then is to explain that after we die there is a judgement, an examination to find out whether we loved Jesus or not. God knows the answer to that but we can be quite sure that no one who loves Jesus can be left out of heaven.

I think that we do need time to explain the relationship between 'me' and 'my body'. The imagery that I use most frequently in this book is the imagery of the tent, because it is a good, clear, biblical image. I live in a tent. You can't really see me because I'm inside. God made this tent for me to live in for the time being. It's like any other tent: it gradually wears out. I'm getting bald and Auntie went quite grey. But it's not really *me* getting old, it's my tent getting old. And one day there may come a big storm and the storm may blow the tent down. That's like an illness. The storm comes and the tent blows down. An illness comes and my body-house dies. But I move out of the tent into the house God has prepared for me (2 Corinthians 5:1). When I move out the body is no longer needed. I'm no longer there to use it. It's finished with.

Do animals go to heaven too? We don't know the answer to that one: 'I don't know the answer to that, but if it would make you happy to have Tigger in heaven with you, then he'll be there. You see, heaven is a *happy* place.'

We may need to explain mourning: 'Then why did you cry when Granny went to heaven?' 'Well, I cried because she was my mummy and she and I had been very happy for forty years. I'm going to miss Granny, and I expect that you will too. I wasn't crying for Granny, you know; *she's* all right. I was sorry for myself.' Once again we shall find our children testing our sincerity. And they will know. Were you really crying for a biblical reason (1 Thessalonians 4:13)?

It is an interesting fact concerning young people in Britain that those between the ages of twelve and twenty have two great fears: a fear that the marriage of their parents is going to crack up, and leave them stranded somewhere in the middle; and the fear of death. If we can wait for the right, the natural moment to explain death to our children, and if we can then actively ask for the Holy Spirit to make our words clear and biblical, then we will be able to give our children tremendous strength, even a kind of *authority* which will make a permanent difference to their lives.

A friend of mine is in hospital, and hasn't been told he is dying. Should I tell him?

No. At least, not yet. Before anyone is told that his illness is 'terminal' it is vital that we get the facts straight. For a start it is essential to consult with the medical people who are caring for him. In the hospital this would include the doctor in charge of the case and the ward Sister. In the home situation it is the patient's own family doctor who ought to be consulted.

These people must be consulted, because while doctors are prepared to warn relatives of the probable outcome of an illness, they are less ready to be dogmatic in many cases as far as telling the patient himself is concerned. The reason for telling and forewarning the relatives is obvious: they need to be prepared and to be given time to clear up any misunderstandings there might be between them, perhaps even to ask some tentative questions of the patient himself. The knowledge can't do *them* any physical harm, and they can sometimes make the decision as to whether or not the patient should himself be told. But to tell the patient himself is a different matter. The knowledge *can* do him physical harm.

In the hospitals, the doctors who come round with their trains of observing student doctors fall into two categories where this question of telling or not telling the patient is concerned: those who will tell the patient and those who won't. And they tend to be rather fixed in their opinions. What's more, they expect that other doctors who serve on their teams should keep whatever their own particular practice happens to be. We must accept the fact that the experienced doctor usually *does* know more about a patient's likely response to the knowledge that death is near than anyone other than a really close relative. And even close relatives often can do no more than *guess*. The trouble is that doctors know that some people simply can't cope with this kind of knowledge. They go to pieces.

A Christian doctor once shared with me an experience which still troubled her. During her Residency she was accompanying the Consultant on his rounds one day. They stopped at the bed of a patient who was suffering from cancer. Everyone in the group of doctors and nurses knew this, but the patient did not know. The Consultant asked a few questions and made a rather cursory examination of the patient and then moved on without saying much to him. But then as the group moved on, my friend remained behind just to be with the patient for a moment. And the patient suddenly blurted out: 'I've got cancer, haven't I? Tell me! It *is* cancer, isn't it?' My doctor friend was completely taken by surprise, was quite unprepared for the question, and almost without thinking told him the fact: yes, he *did* have cancer. From that moment the patient simply went to pieces. He couldn't take the knowledge, even though he had asked for it.

This story fits in here because of the conflict in the evidence offered about whether patients want to be told if they have a terminal illness or not. In survey after survey the results seem to be the same: the doctors, or at any rate a large majority of the doctors, say that the patients *don't* want to know. The patients, or at any rate a large majority of the patients, say that they *do* want to know. But we must be careful how we interpret these survey results. There is a great deal of difference between wanting to know before being told that your illness is *not* terminal, and wanting to know before being told that your illness *is* terminal. What the patients seem to be saying is that they are often unsure of the likely outcome of their illnesses, and if the prospects are *good* they would like to know that. Whether they would *really* want to know if the outlook is bad is another matter. In other words, the patient who has been told that his illness is *not* terminal is glad to have the uncertainty removed. The patient who has been told that his illness *is* terminal may wish that the uncertainty had not been removed. In fact we don't really know whether or not we want to know until we know. And then it's too late.

But two things may be said straight away. Firstly, doctors are on the whole open-minded on the subject of telling the patient the facts about his illness, and will always discuss the matter with a relative or friend of the patient in a sympathetic way. Obviously a doctor could only discuss the patient's case with those who have a legitimate concern. Secondly, most patients who are dying (and some researchers would go even further, and say *all* patients who are dying) know it. It is not entirely clear how they know it. Possibly from within themselves they can sense the change. Possibly from the way in which their visitors behave towards them . . . but somehow they usually seem to know.

So far we have only looked at the question from the practical standpoint. There is a very real theological issue here. The patient surely has a right to know, and a need to know, if he is dying. To put myself right with God, and to put myself right with my family, my friends, even my enemies, must surely be my concern at the end of this life. But the usual conspiracy of silence, or even worse, the usual foggy-cloud of vague hopes and expectations, denies me the chance of dealing with this final act of life here in the way that I should. The act of dying is unique. It is an experience I cannot repeat. It marks the end of one mode of life and the beginning of another. From the Bible we know that there is no coming back here to put things right. The story told by Jesus (Luke 16:19–31) about the rich

man and Lazarus (it is *not* called a parable and since it is not
so called I prefer to treat it as history, as an account of a real
event) depicts three places: the place where the rich man is, the
place where Lazarus is and the earth that both have left behind.
The rich man is now only too well aware of the totally wrong
view of life that he had while he was on the earth. He would
desperately like to go back to earth to give his five brothers a
very different kind of example from the one he had in fact given.
But he can't go back. The die is cast, for him.

This story is an important one because it makes very clear
both the reality of the final separation of forgiven sinner and
the unrepentant sinner, and it makes clear the one-way finality
of death itself. Considerations of this kind may not mean very
much to some doctors. But whether the patient is a Christian
or not it does seem vital that he should be aware of the real
position and be given the opportunity of getting right. And while
we would share the concerns of the doctors for the well-being
of the patient we might have a long-term concern for the well-
being of the patient, eternally, that the doctor cannot share.

But. Surely if we do have relatives and friends who are not
Christians, have we not already shared with them our knowledge
of God; what we know of his marvellous forgiveness? We simply
can't rely on being given the opportunity of a lengthy last illness
during which to open the subject. If we are really convinced
of the truth of the good news about Jesus there won't really
be any difficulty when a relative of ours is taken seriously ill.
He'll *expect* us to talk about Jesus, because that has been the
burden of our conversation all along.

Here is a great problem in the church in Britain, that religion
has become something to be talked about once the grave is in
sight, but not before. But Christianity is all about life! It's
wonderful when an elderly person comes to Christ at the end
of life, but what a shame ... all the wasted years! And what
a risk ... an accident, a heart attack, and life can be over with
no opportunity for a last-minute search for God:

Seek the Lord while he may be found, call upon him while he is
near; let the wicked forsake his way, and the unrighteous man

his thoughts; let him return to the Lord, that he may have mercy on him, and to our God, for he will abundantly pardon (Isaiah 55:6–7).

That verse haunts me. Some years ago an aircraft took off from Addis Ababa airport with a couple of hundred people on board. Most of them had been visiting friends in Ethiopia for the Easter holidays. The plane crashed on take-off. A good many people were killed outright and many others were injured. Some knew that they were dying. There were plenty of Christian nurses in Addis Ababa who went out to help in the rescue operation. And again and again the comment was the same: they found people who *wanted* to get right with God, but they had left him out all through their lives. And they had left it too late. We just didn't seem to be able to get through to some of them.

So, yes, there is a theological reason for letting someone who is dying know the position. The doctor will rightly be concerned to ensure that nothing is said that would hinder the patient's recovery. But if we are really concerned then our concern will normally have shown itself long before a terminal illness.

One more point. Christians need to prepare for death, too. There aren't too many of us who take seriously the brevity of life. We should ourselves always be ready: disagreements cleared up as we go along, finances kept in order, all necessary paper work organized, a will made. I recall a missionary friend of mine being taken into hospital with a serious brain haemorrhage. His wife was with him and so was I. Just before he lapsed into a coma, a coma from which he never regained consciousness, his wife leaned across and asked him if there was anything she could do for him: 'You know that you are very ill. Is there anything you want done? Call someone? Write a letter, maybe?' Graham thought for a moment or two, and then said: 'No, nothing.' He had so lived his life that to the best of his knowledge he had kept short accounts with us all. There were no last minute adjustments to be made. He was ready to go.

Not all of us live like that. So, if we are able to bear it, we need to be told that the end of the journey is near, so that we can get right with God and get right with one another.

I've just learned that I have only a year to live. How should I spend this time?

People who have been asked this question in a hypothetical way have given all the usual answers. Some of them have said that they would sell up and go on a world tour. Others would spend such time as was left in prayer. Or others would take the opportunity of doing all the things they have always intended doing, but never got around to. But there's a great deal of difference between giving the answer to a hypothetical question and trying to face up to the real situation. One man who was given only three months to live commented: 'I shall carry on as usual, but I shall probably extract more pleasure from the little things of life than I have done in the past.'

Actually we do have some biblical advice to give on this question. When Isaiah told King Hezekiah that he was going to die, he began by telling Hezekiah, 'Set your house in order' (2 Kings 20:1). So at least we should set about that task: set your house in order.

But on second thoughts, why should we set the house in order? After all we won't be there to worry about things. If our finances are chaotic what can it possibly matter to us? If the family is not provided for why should we worry? We won't be there.

True; but we shall be somewhere. Death is not the end. The effects of our lives go on long past the point at which we 'die'; and not only the effects. We go on. This points up one aspect of living in the expectation of death: far from becoming more self-centred, we who are Christians should become more concerned for others. Set your house in order! How is my husband going to cope? How can I make it easier for my wife when I have gone? How will the rest of the family manage? Will they be able to find all the bits of paper they will need to tidy up my affairs? What about my business? Is everyone cared for?

Isaiah's words to Hezekiah seem to carry this message: when we know that we have only a short way to go we should not spend the time left to us on ourselves, but on others. So what *you* should do I don't know. But I suspect that you will be more kind, more affectionate, more gentle, more considerate, more ... well, more like Jesus.

Which is a reminder. In a sense we are all in the same boat. We none of us have long to live. The man who is told he has six months to live knows roughly how long he has, but then we too know roughly how long we are likely to live. So that I, too, should be looking at the quality of my life, to see how it looks in the certainty of death. In the certainty of eternity.

This concept of living my life *now* in the awareness of eternity is an important one. The Bible tells us that whoever believes in Jesus *has* eternal life. Notice the Bible insistence that he has it, not that he is going to get it. Eternal life is God's free gift to his people. But what is eternal life? It is much more than life that goes on for ever. It is the life of eternity, the kind of life that is demanded by the concept of eternity. And what does that mean? Well, eternity is God's dwelling place (Isaiah 57:15). What kind of life is suited to God's home? I would think that all values are changed there. What means so much here won't mean too much there; as Jesus put it, the first will be last and the last will be first (Matthew 19:30). That seems to mean that the important people 'down here' may not mean too much 'up there'. So presumably the approval and praise of people here won't count for too much there.

And then, in the light of eternity all the things that so regularly do go wrong in life look so different. Even a broken leg seems a different matter when looked at from the standpoint of eternity. Even a broken heart looks different from the standpoint of eternity. It is this outlook that enables martyrs to stand up for God, to give up their lives. In a quieter way it's the standpoint of eternity that gives us a proper balance for our everyday lives. A broken cup and saucer isn't worth a flaming row with the children, a missed birthday no reason for ending a friendship.

The fact is that we all know that we are going to die. The

doctors don't need to tell us. And we should all be living, all the time, the life of eternity which we have ... if we have Christ (John 6:47 and 1 John 15:12).

Is dying painful?

Paul comments simply: 'The sting of death is sin' (1 Corinthians 15:56). The pain of death does not lie in the act of dying. All the evidence that we have shows that death itself, dying, is not painful. But sin, the whole weight of the realization of a life wasted, maybe even a whole life lived out in open defiance of God ... that can well make death painful.

The Bible also suggests that the *expectation* of death, the anticipation of it, trying to imagine it, maybe even resisting it, may be painful. In 1 Samuel 15:32–33 we have the Amalekite leader Agag brought to Samuel for execution. He has been expecting this ever since his capture by Saul. But in the waiting time he has come to terms with it. He must die, but he's no longer afraid of it: 'Surely the bitterness of death is past.'

The words used in the Bible to describe death would also suggest to us that for the Christian, whose sins are forgiven, death is not painful. We have already seen that death can be seen as 'falling asleep' (Acts 7:60). When Paul was in his last imprisonment, expecting death at any time, he wrote to Timothy: 'the time of my departure has come' (2 Timothy 4:6). He was setting off on a journey: at the end of one, rather tiring road, but at the beginning of another. He certainly doesn't give any impression of fearing the move.

But it must be recognized that some illnesses do bring a great deal of pain, and in such cases the long drawn-out sufferings of a final illness can be really tough. In fact there is probably no harder experience to pass through than to sit with a person, especially with a child, who has some painful and yet extended terminal disease.

Even the emotional suffering can be very great. I found it immensely difficult to bear the final weeks in the life of a doctor friend of mine. She had given her life to work in Ethiopia. In fact she went to Ethiopia originally at the personal request of the old Emperor, Haile Selassie. Margaret was a gynaecologist. And then she added leprosy to her specialities and worked in a mission leprosy hospital and later in a Government leprosy hospital. So closely did she identify with her patients that she was rarely separated from them. Near the end she contracted leprosy. She still had it when she died.

But Margaret didn't die of leprosy. She had a brain haemorrhage. She rapidly became unconscious, and when she recovered consciousness she had completely lost the power of speech or movement. Her mind was as clear as ever. When I first got to her she had worked out a system of spelling out words through tapping, and as I walked in she at once tapped out, 'He must have some tea'! But that movement went. Totally. She lingered on for about a fortnight. And I still recall how she would drift off to sleep, and then gradually wake up ... and her eyes would fill with tears as she found herself *wanting* so desperately to communicate with us, to say something, but found that she couldn't.

Others have had much more difficult experiences than that. But I found it terribly hard to accept. *Why* should there be such suffering? And I still don't have the answer. There is no simple answer to pain and sorrow and suffering. Except for this: this is not the world as God meant it to be. It is not even the world as God intends that one day it will be. Our alienation from God, man's sin and selfishness, man's rebellion, which means that God's will is *not* done on earth as it is in heaven, all these things make life what it is. And there has to be an answer to it. At some time it must be put right. The Bible tells me that it *will* be put right.

Until then, death may be a painful experience, painful because of the nature of the illness, painful simply to share. But still it must be said again, death itself, dying, is not painful. Of course, most people are under medical care when they die, either in hospital or at home. And doctors are now able to cope with pain: it really isn't necessary to fear intolerable pain. And in addition to the help that doctors can give there is also God's own provision, the body's kindly anaesthetic that seems to take over towards the end of life here.

However, some people really do experience 'death'. They are able to remain fully conscious right to the end-of-the-beginning, the end of this life which is the beginning of the next. Such people, if Christians, seem to experience great peace, and even great excitement as life here draws to a close. The one account of dying which has really stuck in my mind comes from Dr Leslie Weatherhead. He wrote:

> I have sat at the bedside of a man who was dying and conscious to the end. He gripped my hand, and I must have gripped his more tightly than I thought I was doing, for he said, 'Don't hold me back. I can see through the gates. It's marvellous!'

Victor Solow's own account of his 'death' was published by *Reader's Digest* in 1975, and again confirms that death itself is not painful. On March 23rd 1974 Victor went for a run and at 10.52 he suffered cardiac arrest: his heart simply stopped beating. For twenty-three minutes he was clinically dead. Others breathed for him. He wrote of just how difficult he found it to describe his experience because when he 'died' he left his normal senses behind him in the 'dead' body. He had new senses, but they didn't relate to the old ones and he could not find the vocabulary with which to describe the new sensations. Of his death he wrote:

> For me, the moment of transition from life to death – what else can one call it – was easy. There was no time for fear, pain or thought ... there was no pain. The sensation was neither pleasant nor unpleasant, but completely consuming.

Solow also commented on his self-awareness, on his discovery of a new 'I':

> This new 'I' was not the 'I' that I knew, but rather a distilled essence of it, yet somehow vaguely familiar, something I had always known, buried under a superstructure of personal fears, hopes, wants and needs.

Actually many people have had similar experiences and have been able to describe them in some detail. Often they can comment on seeing their bodies lying in bed while they hovered somewhere above. However, a similar experience can be induced by drugs, and what is more important it is obvious that people who described these experiences had not, in fact, died. If they had, they wouldn't be here telling us about the experience. But still it is interesting that people who have gone right to the very brink of death, and then come back again, have agreed that dying itself is not painful.

One final word. Professor Sir Norman Anderson was taking part in a television programme devised by Malcolm Muggeridge, and called *Why God?* Others involved in the programme included a rabbi, a nun, a Muslim and a Buddhist, as well as Baroness Wootton, who does not believe in God. She particularly pilloried the notion of a God of love who allows suffering. Sir Norman Anderson responded with the dying words of his own son, who had only recently died of cancer:

I am going to my Lord.

We do *not* understand the mystery of suffering. But I believe that one day we shall:

Not till the loom is silent and the shuttles cease to fly
Shall God unroll the canvas and explain the reason why.
The dark threads are as needful in the Weaver's skilful hand
As the threads of gold and silver in the pattern He has planned.

3

THE BODY AFTER DEATH

What is the purpose of a funeral?

The funeral service has not one, but at least four important functions. First of all it is for the *reverent* disposal of a body which is no longer needed. In dealing with the last question I commented that the human body is not 'vile', although it is frail. The human body was marvellously made by God. It is the tent in which we live for maybe fifty, sixty or more years.

At the funeral service we are dealing with the cast-off tent of one whom we loved. God made it, and so, on two counts, it is to be treated with respect. No matter where you go in the world you will find that all societies have special ceremonies which ensure that these discarded tents *are* treated with respect.

But there is a second purpose behind the funeral service, a psychological purpose. When someone we have known and loved for many years is taken from us we may find it very difficult to accept the fact. Some relatives *refuse* to accept the fact and will continue to act as though the one who has died is still alive, and likely to turn up at any moment. His place may be set at meal time, his clothes kept pressed and cleaned, his bed carefully made, his books or typewriter kept ready. Clearly this is an unhealthy condition for any person to be in. The funeral service provides a definite end-point to the relationship, the incontrovertible evidence that he has gone. It is often precisely when a relative refuses to attend the funeral service that the unhealthy refusal to come to terms with the death is found.

The funeral of a Christian has another purpose. The two

purposes I have mentioned above are common to all funerals. But when a Christian dies there is a tremendous opportunity to explain to those who attend the funeral exactly what Christians believe about death. Death is the great question mark over our lives. If we have the answer to it, what better place can there be for giving the answer than at the funeral service?

When I first went to Ethiopia as a missionary I was sent away to study the language. While I was in language school I saw my first Ethiopian funeral. It was not a Christian funeral. There were hundreds of mourners present. The body was carried ahead of the long wailing procession. The close relatives walked just behind the plain wooden coffin. I recall that it was a young boy who had died. His mother was amongst the mourners. Following the funeral customs of her people she leaped and she wept and she screamed and she tore at her face until the blood came. She was joined by the other women, sometimes in a vortex of leaping, wailing, bleeding, suffering humanity. I never forgot that sight.

A few months later I was sent to my first appointment. I was teaching in a school run primarily for the children of the thousands of Christians who lived in the area. Shortly after I got there an old grandmother died. Of course I attended the funeral: I had been in the country long enough to know that attendance at funerals was expected of all who even remotely knew the one who had died. I rather expected something like the other funeral that I had seen. But what a contrast! I waited in a field beside a rough pathway and in the distance I could hear singing. The funeral procession wound its way towards me: no crying, no leaping around, no despair. No, the missionaries had not interfered with local custom. The Christians themselves had worked out their own thanatology, their own doctrine of death. They knew that their faith in Christ had totally transformed the situation.

I would go further. Again and again, in conversation with older Ethiopian Christians, I found that *first* in any list of what Christ had done for them was just this: deliverance from the fear of death. And so the procession came through the fields, singing. No, it wasn't *Onward Christian Soldiers* translated into the Hadya language, but a hymn of their own creation. At the graveside the hundreds of mourners gathered round, while one of the elders preached, explaining so simply why they weren't all weeping. That was an unforgettable experience, a vivid illustration of the difference that Christ makes. But what kind of a testimony is it if there is no difference between the funeral of a Christian and that of someone who had no trust in God?

I believe that people do want to hear what we have to say about this matter of death. I remember being in Westminster Hospital some years ago. In the bed next to me was a man who was awaiting surgery for a brain tumour. He had undergone surgery once before and now this terrible thing was back again. He was a highly intelligent man and he knew quite well what the possibilities were. He might be cured. He might die during the operation. He might recover from the operation but find himself paralysed. We got talking and he soon discovered that I was a Christian. I could sense his nervousness: he *wanted* to discuss this real possibility, death, but would I talk sense or mere theological gobbledygook?

I asked him:

'Do you want to talk about this thing, death?'

'Yes, I do.'

Now it happened that my wife had just made a mistake. I had asked her to bring some cassettes in for me: I wanted to do some editing, I think. And she had brought the 'wrong' ones. Amongst them was the recording of a sermon I had preached, a broadcast talk, actually, on what Christians believe about death. I offered it to him. He took it, and my tape recorder, drew the curtains round his bed and listened to it. Afterwards we talked again:

> I have listened to the church services on the radio, and I have gone to church myself, but this is the first time that anything that has been said has made sense.

We talked a deal more, and became good friends. No, he didn't die, but made a recovery that astonished the ward sister (as she herself admitted to me). We were soon separated, for I had to go back to Africa again, although I've heard from him since. But those words still ring in my ears, 'the first time that anything that has been said has made sense'. On this subject we *must* make sense.

So, the funeral service is meant to be a reverent disposal of the tent which is no longer needed, and it is a means of making plain the final break in what might have been a long and close relationship. But it is also an opportunity for explaining what Christ has done for us: that for Christians the separation is not final. Peter advises us:

> Always be prepared to give an answer to everyone who asks you to give the reason for the hope that you have (1 Peter 3:15, New International Version);

and the funeral service is certainly one time when that answer should be given.

Finally, I would have thought that the funeral service should be an opportunity for showing how the life now ended here has been used to God's glory. I attended a funeral service not long ago and was shocked to notice that throughout the service there was no reference, except indirectly, to the one who had died. Not even her name was mentioned. That saddened me. I like to think of a Christian funeral service as *a service of thanksgiving for the life of the one who has died*. I would expect the one who is conducting the funeral service to find out something about the life of the one who has died, and to show us something of how God worked in that life.

I'm not going to deny the reality of sorrow at a funeral. We are sorry for ourselves because long years of friendship are temporarily ended. But it's all just temporary. We will come together again, where there will be no more partings. And putting aside our sorrows, there really is something rather wonderful about the end of the journey, for a Christian: safe home at last!

Can you suggest some hymns suitable for a Christian funeral?

This isn't really a question about *the Bible*, but still I'll try to respond with some biblically sound hymns. And that's not as simple as it sounds: so many hymns are sentimental and earnest, but for all that not biblical.

Some of us have long remembered and cherished the hymns which were sung at the funeral of Sir Winston Churchill, especially this one:

> Mine eyes have seen the glory of the coming of the Lord,
> He is trampling out the vintage where the grapes of wrath are stored,
> He hath loosed the fateful lightning of his terrible swift sword,
> Our God is marching on!

The third verse is particularly relevant:

> He has sounded forth the trumpet that shall never call retreat,
> He is sifting out the hearts of men before his judgement seat;
> Oh be swift my soul to answer him, be jubilant my feet!
> Our God is marching on!

Incidentally I have long cherished the story that came out of Billy Graham's famous meeting with Sir Winston. After they had talked together for very much longer than had been scheduled, Sir Winston asked Billy Graham: 'Well, am I converted now?' to which Billy Graham replied, sensitively, 'No, sir, but I think you are convicted!'

Certainly the most commonly sung hymn at funerals is one or other setting of the twenty-third psalm, usually to the tune 'Crimond':

> The Lord's my shepherd, I'll not want,
> He makes me down to lie in pastures green,
> He leadeth me the quiet waters by.
>
> Yea, though I walk through death's dark vale
> Yet will I fear no ill, for Thou art with me,
> And Thy rod and staff me comfort still.

The paraphrase *The King of Love* is often chosen:

> The King of Love my shepherd is
> Whose goodness faileth never,
> I nothing lack if I am his
> And he is mine for ever.
>
> In death's dark vale I fear no ill,
> With Thee dear Lord beside me;
> Thy rod and staff my comfort still,
> Thy cross before to guide me.

Another hymn very commonly asked for is Henry Francis Lyte's *Abide With Me*:

> Abide with me, fast falls the eventide;
> The darkness deepens, Lord with me abide;
> When other helpers fail and comforts flee,
> Help of the helpless, O abide with me!
>
> Swift to its close ebbs out life's little day;
> Earth's joys grow dim, its glories pass away;
> Change and decay in all around I see –
> O Thou who changest not, abide with me.

This particular hymn is, of course, a meditation on Luke 24:29 –

> But they constrained Jesus, saying, 'Abide with us; for it is toward evening, and the day is far spent.'

The hymn is still sounded out across Torbay from the bells at the church where Francis Lyte was a much beloved minister for a lifetime. However, it must be confessed that the original words do *not* refer to the shadows of death, but perhaps they may be allowed to stand since they do appear in the context of Christ's resurrection.

Abide With Me and *The Lord's My Shepherd* are a reminder that we often find people at a funeral service although they do not normally attend church. It is wise to remember this when choosing hymns for a funeral. Often a hymn that was once much loved but has long been forgotten can open the heart of the listener in a way that no number of sermons might do. For example, John Bunyan's old hymn *He who would valiant be* has an alternative first verse which, together with the usual third verse, gives a very suitable funeral hymn for a Christian:

Who would true valour see, let him come hither;
One here will constant be, come wind, come weather;
There's no discouragement shall make him once relent
His first avowed intent to be a pilgrim.

Since, Lord, Thou dost defend us with Thy Spirit,
We know we at the end shall life inherit.
Then fancies flee away! I'll fear not what men say,
I'll labour night and day to be a pilgrim.

The hymn *O God, Our Help in Ages Past* is very suitable as far as the words are concerned, but the tune is rather mournful. To my mind one of the most thrilling of all hymns is the great song of praise *For All the Saints*. I was very hesitant about this hymn until eventually I sat down to read it through, when I discovered what I should have known all along. This hymn is a hymn of thanksgiving for the lives of the people of God now safe home with the King, and not some kind of musical 'prayer for the dead'. I've sung it with real thanksgiving ever since:

For all the saints, who from their labours rest,
Who Thee, by faith, before the world confessed,
Thy name O Jesus, be for ever blessed. Hallelujah!

Thou wast their Rock, their Fortress and their Might;
Thou, Lord, their Captain in the well fought fight;
Thou in the darkness drear, their one true Light. Hallelujah!

There's a word of encouragement in the middle of the hymn for those who are still engaged in the battle for our faith:

And when the strife is fierce, the warfare long,
Steals on the ear the distant triumph song,
And hearts are brave again, and arms are strong. Hallelujah!

The last verse, with its picture of the millions of God's people at last thronging into the heavenly Jerusalem, is thrilling beyond measure:

> From earth's wide bounds, from ocean's farthest coast,
> Through gates of pearl streams in the countless host,
> Singing to Father, Son and Holy Ghost – Hallelujah!

I was reminded of this great hymn recently when I was able to visit Ethiopia to teach the Bible at the annual United Church Leaders' Conference. There were Christian leaders there, from all over Ethiopia, leaders of all the denominations, all differences laid aside. At the end of the conference there was a Communion service. Three or four of the church leaders stood at the front of the building where the meetings were being held. I sat behind them and watched the lines of Christians as they came forward to receive bread and wine. A young girl, who until a few weeks before had been a Muslim, now the only Christian in her village, came shyly forward. Then an old evangelist: I had known him for many years as a faithful preacher-missionary; an Addis Ababa pastor; a member of the choir; a girl from the Pentecostal church who had spent weeks in prison for her faith; a Bible school teacher and elder, imprisoned no fewer than eight times for Christ. On they came, hundreds of them, and the tears rolled down my cheeks as I watched . . . I could almost *see* them moving forward, always forward, up to the heavenly gates themselves. 'For all the saints . . . Thy Name, O Jesus, be for ever blessed, Hallelujah!'

The grand old hymn *The Sands of Time are Sinking* is very suitable, but not too many people know it nowadays. A beautifully simple and comforting hymn is *Peace, Perfect Peace*:

> Peace, perfect peace, with sorrows surging round?
> In Jesus' presence naught but calm is found.
>
> Peace, perfect peace, with loved ones far away?
> In Jesus' bosom we are safe and they.
>
> Peace, perfect peace, death shadowing us and ours?
> Jesus has vanquished death and all its powers.

Of course there are many more. *When I Survey the Wondrous Cross* directs attention to the place where salvation was worked out for us and to the person who worked it out. Hymns about heaven such as *Jerusalem the Golden* and *How Bright these Glorious Spirits Shine* are obviously suitable.

And then there are the hymns which look forward to our Lord's return. The Christian hope is clearly expressed in that great hymn *Lo! He Comes*:

> Lo! He comes with clouds descending,
> Once for favoured sinners slain,
> Thousand thousand saints attending
> Swell the triumph of His train:
> Hallelujah!
> Christ appears on earth to reign.
>
> Now redemption, long expected,
> See in solemn pomp appear!
> All His saints, by man rejected,
> Now shall meet Him in the air.
> Hallelujah!
> See the day of God appear.

Charles Wesley wrote it and as usual he provides us with sung scripture!

Is it wrong to grieve when someone dies?

It seems to me that if we really understand what the Bible has to say about death and the Christian, the *quality* of our grieving will be changed. But the Bible suggests that it is not wrong to grieve.

If we go back to the records that we have of life in the early church we find that the first Christians certainly grieved when one of them died. In Acts 9:36–43 we have the account of Peter's visit to Joppa, where a woman named Tabitha lived. She is described as a disciple, a believer, and we are told that she was marked out by her charity, her many thoughtful acts. Tabitha fell sick and died. When this happened, the other disciples did not simply rejoice that she was so soon safely home with the Lord. They obviously regretted that so useful a member of the church should be taken from them prematurely. They didn't satisfy themselves with merely regretting her death: they sent two men to call Peter from nearby Lydda. Their message was peremptory: 'Come without delay.' And when Peter arrived he found, not a state of holiday, but an experience of widespread grief: 'All the widows stood beside him weeping ...' (verse 39). For his part, Peter did not merely tell them to buck up their ideas a bit and behave like Christians. He set about interceding with God for her restoration to that life in which she had so obviously been useful to the church. And finally, God, for his part, did not refuse Peter's request, nor did he send an angelic messenger to explain to them the doctrine of death, but he restored Tabitha to them.

The reaction on the part of the various friends of Tabitha was very natural, even for Christians. True enough *Tabitha* was all right. She had possibly been in a great deal of pain because of her illness and now she was safe with her Lord. We must remember that those days were hard for those who were sick. There was little understanding of how the body worked and even less of the way in which diseases attacked the body. Little could be done to relieve pain. So that it would be easy to rationalize the whole experience of death and accept the fact that Tabitha was well out of this world, safe with Jesus.

But that isn't the whole story. It is true that most of our grief at such times of bereavement is for ourselves. One does grieve for a husband and wife separated after many years together, for parents who lose a child, for children who lose mother or father. Death continues to be the 'last enemy' (1 Corinthians 15:26).

And then again, some funerals are really tough. For some years I was the Minister of the International Church in Addis Ababa. During those years I conducted quite a number of funeral services and several of them were difficult for me. One was particularly hard. An Australian doctor, a comparatively young man, had only recently joined us to help with the famine situation in the Ogaden area of eastern Ethiopia. This area borders Somalia, and is largely inhabited by Somali people. The Somalis are almost all of them Muslims.

Douglas took his skills into this desert region, accepting the really primitive conditions in which they all had to live. Obviously there was very little water for them, there were no roads, no shops, since the Somali people are largely nomadic. Early one morning they set up camp in a remote region of a new area, and Douglas set about the task of preparing for his surgery. And while he was busily working a fanatical Muslim came up behind him and plunged a knife into his back. Douglas died instantly.

The nurses who were with him escaped from the murderer who had actually turned on them, and eventually they were able to bring Douglas' body out, after a nightmare journey in a Land Rover. They flew back with the body to Addis Ababa.

I was in the church before the funeral. Sitting at the front were two of the nurses who had been with Douglas when it had all happened. They were trying not to cry, and yet they couldn't help it. And I had to say to them as I had to say to some other missionaries, all brought up on the tradition that the Christian doesn't weep at the funeral of another Christian, I had to say to them: 'Go on, cry! Of course it's sad. Of course it's a tragedy. Why pretend otherwise?' So they wept, and released the tensions and the sadness that were inevitable.

Douglas was gone. It was sad to see all the plans Douglas had made for the future suddenly ended. It was sad to think of his parents, back in Australia, looking forward to seeing him again in just a few weeks, and now they wouldn't be seeing him. It was sad to see the result of man's hatred, hatred for someone who only wanted the chance to do him good.

But don't cry for Douglas.

We had many people at that funeral service. There were representatives of the Ethiopian government and there were people from the embassies. And several of them commented afterwards on the completely new light that the service had shed on the real meaning of the Christian faith. Of course we grieved, but it was not grief such as I had seen at so many funerals. It was not the grief of hopelessness, of despair. It was sorrow for what *we* had lost, we his friends, his co-workers, his family. But in death we had not come to the end of our resources. In Christ we have an explanation of death; death itself is redeemed. We are not to grieve as if we have no expectation of ever meeting again. But still, death is a parting. And partings are sad.

Paul put it very simply:

> But we would not have you ignorant, brethren, concerning those who are asleep, that you may not grieve *as others do* who have no hope. For since we believe that Jesus died and rose again, even so, through Jesus, God will bring with him those who have fallen asleep (1 Thessalonians 4:13–14).

Let me close by saying that if someone does feel very deeply the loss of some very close friend, then it can be very dangerous *not* to weep. Out of a wrong idea that it's totally wrong to weep or grieve, some people do bottle their grief up, and may even cultivate a brave smile and a cheerful exterior. Now that's all right if you really feel that way. But if not, and you still bottle up your natural feelings of grief, it is very possible that one day the bottle will explode ... the pent-up feelings will burst out, perhaps against someone for whom you really care, and you may be astonished at the violence of your feelings. Paul does not suggest that we should not grieve; simply that we must not grieve as those who have no hope.

Is cremation wrong for a Christian?

Without doubt cremation is growing in popularity, both in Britain and, to a lesser but increasing degree, in the United States. In Britain today more than sixty per cent of all funerals involve cremation. Incidentally it is interesting to note that Archbishop William Temple's body was cremated in 1944, and amongst others who asked for their bodies to be cremated were Dr W. E. Sangster and Dr G. Campbell Morgan.

Obviously this is an important question. Actually, the Bible doesn't say very much about the way in which we are to deal with the body left behind by the departed soul. However, throughout the Bible there is clear evidence of the need for showing proper respect for the body. On one occasion David departed from this principle: the rather gruesome story is recorded in 2 Samuel 21. He executed seven of Saul's sons, or rather handed them over to be executed, which is much the same thing. But the Gibeonites who carried out the executions took their vengeance beyond death, and instead of allowing the bodies of the seven to be decently buried left them on the gallows. The mother of two of the hanged men, Rizpah, could not bear to see this crude hatred directed at the unresisting bodies of these men. She took up her station beside the gibbets and through long days beat off the carrion birds and the wild animals. Somehow her action was brought to the attention of David, and he was moved by this insistence of hers that the human body cannot be treated with such disrespect. He arranged for the disgusting spectacle to be ended and for the bodies to be given a proper burial.

Burial was the normal way of disposing of the body in Old Testament times, although it was not burial as we know it; not burial in a hole in the ground, but burial in a cave. We can go right back to Genesis 23 and the story of the death of Abraham's wife Sarah to find this practice being observed. Abraham bought a field in Machpelah, a field which belonged to Ephron, but he bought it for the sake of a cave in that field:

> After this, Abraham buried Sarah his wife in the cave of the field of Machpelah (Genesis 23:19).

When Abraham died he was buried in the same cave (Genesis 25:7-10).

In the New Testament we find the same practice: burial in a cave. There is also mention of the body being anointed with oils and spices before being wrapped in some kind of linen covering and being placed in the grave, which would then be closed by a large stone. In Jerusalem, in the Tombs of the Kings, not far from Gordon's Calvary, we can still see just such a cave burial chamber, with the rolling stone still in its groove.

The Bible does not make direct mention of cremation as being a normal means for the disposal of the dead. However, there are at least four references to the burning of the dead. Amos records the Lord's displeasure with the Moabites because they had burned the bones of the king of Edom: his judgement took the form of fire to devour them as fire had devoured the bones of the Edomite king. The suggestion here is that the Edomite king had died and been properly buried, but that his Moabite enemies then disinterred the body to take a crude vengeance upon it by burning the bones: possibly even as a sacrifice to their gods (Amos 2:1–3).

Judges 15:6 may refer to a similar action on the part of the Philistines, but it seems much more likely that they simply burned down the house of Samson's father-in-law, and both his father-in-law and his wife died in the blaze.

The third case of the burning of the body occurs in Joshua 7:25, in the context of the story of Achan's disobedience. Despite the ban on looting during the capture of Jericho, Achan had managed to get away with a considerable quantity of loot which he hid in his tent. He was executed for his crime, his body was then burned and a cairn of stones finally erected over the site. This departure from the normal practice of burial in a cave is an indication of the judgement of God; it was, perhaps, parallel to the old practice of burying executed murderers within the confines of the prison at which the execution took place and in 'unconsecrated ground'.

Fourthly, in 1 Samuel 31 we have a very different case, that of the burning of the bodies of Saul and his sons who were killed by the Philistines. The bodies were abused by the Philistines: Saul's head was cut off, and his armour stripped from him, while his body was nailed to the wall of Beth-shan. The inhabitants of the town of Jabesh Gilead heard what had happened and then:

all the valiant men arose, and went all night, and took the body
of Saul and the bodies of his sons from the wall of Beth-shan; and
they came to Jabesh and burnt them there. And they took their
bones and buried them under the tamarisk tree in Jabesh, and fasted
seven days (1 Samuel 31:12–13).

That this cremation followed by the respectful burial of the
bones of Saul and his sons met with David's approval is apparent
from 2 Samuel 2:5–6:

May you be blessed by the Lord, because you showed this loyalty
to Saul your lord, and buried him.

It is not quite clear why they cremated the bodies before burying
them; almost certainly the reason was that they feared the
Philistines might have followed them, might discover the graves,
disinter the bodies and subject them to further indignities.
(Incidentally, it is worth noting that the New English Bible
removes the cremation from the story altogether, translating
'anointed them' instead of 'burned them'. The later Good News
Bible, however, returns to the more usual translation.)

These four accounts of burnings may be set alongside the
teaching in Leviticus which made the burning of the body a
symbol of divine judgement. In Leviticus 20:14 it is laid down
that if a man marries a woman, and then also marries her mother,
apparently with the approval of the daughter, all three were
to be burned. The same sentence was to be passed on the
daughter of a priest if she became a prostitute (Leviticus 21:9).
These six passages all seem to share a concern, the concern
that the body of one who has died should be treated with respect,
and that where the living person was, for some horrendous
reason, placed beyond the pale, then, and then only, as a symbol
of judgement the body might be burned. But subsequently *no
attempt was made to inter the ashes.*

The Bible does appear to be concerned with motives rather
than with methods when it comes to the question of the disposal
of the dead. The Moabites were wrong in burning the body
of the king of Edom not because they burned it, but because
they burned it as a gesture of hatred. The Gileadites, on the

other hand, were right when they burned the body of Saul because their motive·in burning it was right.

On the matter of cremation, our own culture has changed rather rapidly in the last few decades. To a very large extent this is simply due to practical considerations. There has been an irresistible drift towards living in the towns and cities, and there simply isn't enough land available in these sprawling centres of population to make ordinary interment possible for all. So the practice of cremation, usually followed by the dispersal of the ashes, has grown.

There are some people who object to cremation because it does not conform with biblical practice. This argument would have more force if the usual interment followed biblical practice, but of course it doesn't. As we have already seen, in both Old and New Testaments burial was customarily in a cave. Others object on the grounds that cremation represents an attempt to evade the resurrection. That does seem to me rather an odd idea. First of all, very many Christians have been burned to death, some even as martyrs, and one can hardly suppose that such will be excluded from the resurrection. And secondly there is as little left of the body after a few years of burial as there is after a few minutes of burning. And thirdly it does not appear to me to be scriptural to think of the resurrection body as in any sense being put together out of the remnants, incinerated or interred, of the physical body. Provided that the physical body is treated with proper respect the biblical imperatives seem to be observed.

And this brings us to the very practical consideration that cremation is very much less expensive than ordinary interment. It does seem wrong to spend several hundred pounds on buying a burial plot and then paying for some kind of commemorative stone, when for a tenth of that amount the body can be disposed of reverently and in what seems to me to be a Christian way, and a way that is not forbidden by Scripture.

Now there is nothing secret or hidden about the operation of a crematorium. In fact, at most crematoria it is possible to arrange a visit and to be shown round. This is very helpful, because from time to time all kinds of rumours circulate about what goes on in the crematoria.

Two coffins are never incinerated together. The ashes from one cremation are never allowed to be confused with the ashes from another. Every crematorium has its own system for ensuring that the ashes do not, at any point, become confused with those of another cremation. The ashes are carefully collected, and may be scattered by the crematorium officials, or may be interred at a separate service, or may be handed to the relatives to be disposed of in some way that might have been particularly requested.

There are several advantages of cremation over the more traditional burial. I have already mentioned the cost. But a much more important point, to me, is that the service at the crematorium is *very much easier* for the relatives to take than the churchyard service. The chapel itself is always designed to give a sense of tranquillity and restfulness. It is usually vaguely familiar: a kindly combination of Anglican church and Non-conformist chapel with, it seems to me, the good points of both: Anglican dignity, and Non-conformist warmth. Often it will be rather like the church in which we usually worship.

By contrast the churchyard service takes place in the open air, often in most uncomfortable conditions, with wind or rain or even snow, from which there can be little shelter. We are not familiar with the graveyard, or cemetery, and the rows of tombstones are vaguely depressing. The grave itself is inevitably intimidating, in spite of the efforts of the undertaker to conceal the raw earth with his spread of artificial grass.

Of course, where one feels that cremation is wrong, then it is possible for all these disadvantages to be overcome, and the graveside service can be lifted up to a triumphant experience. But it rarely happens like that. Any singing is necessarily thin, and lost in the open air.... No, I have no doubt myself that for its power to witness, for its sense of peace, for its kindness to those who mourn, the crematorium service always has the advantage. But this is of course only my own opinion. Suffice it to say that, as far as the Bible is concerned, there is no reason why bodies should not respectfully be cremated.

Is it right for a Christian to donate, say, his kidneys for surgical transplant?

My first response is not particularly helpful: every Christian has to make up his own mind about this. We just can't produce any rules because the Bible doesn't even consider the possibility of surgical transplants. But perhaps we can think about the principles involved and try to work out some kind of guidance.

First of all, we have been using right through this book the concept of a body which is in many respects like a tent. It can be thought of as something that 'I' live in. It literally changes from moment to moment, as old cells die off and are flaked away, and new cells are built up by the marvellous chemistry of the body. But the body inevitably gets older, and it tends to wear out. From time to time it is attacked by disease. When this happens it may manage to recover by itself, or I may have to bring in outside help: the doctor's medicines. The drugs that I take do affect the whole body. They may be used to lower my temperature, slow down my heart beat, stimulate my gastric juices or any number of other things.

We have also become accustomed to surgery, something one step further on from medicine. The surgeon may actually interfere with the parts of the tent, shortening the ropes, patching up the canvas or perhaps strengthening the tent pole. That is to say he may have to amputate a leg, provide me with a skin graft or set a fractured bone.

Any of these activities, medical or surgical, may have quite drastic effects on my life style. For example, some people's stomachs produce too much acid and this may lead to ulcers. If a person like that gets caught in a traffic jam he can actually *feel* the acid pumping into his stomach, he can *feel* the tension building up. But if the vagus nerve of such a person is cut it may so reduce the flow of acid that the very same person will be able to sit in a traffic jam and not feel any tension at all.

He may even enjoy it! Perfect calm. People may admire him for it! But it's just spin-off from surgery.

So we are quite accustomed to having doctors re-arrange the bits and pieces of our bodies in an effort towards making them function better.

But nowadays the doctors are able to go one stage further. They can actually run a kind of spare-parts service. At the moment this is a rather limited service, but even if it is limited it has already meant a completely new kind of life for some people. What is entailed is simply the transfer of a healthy organ from one person, the donor, to someone else, the recipient. Of course the process isn't just as straightforward as patching up an old dress. There are all the problems of matching tissues, and coping with rejection responses, and many of these problems are still not properly understood. But the fact is that some people are alive today because they have had a diseased organ replaced by a healthy one from a donor. Very many people are able to see because the diseased corneas in their eyes have been replaced by healthy ones from donors.

Sometimes it is possible to take the healthy organ from a living donor. It appears to be quite possible to live comfortably with only one kidney, so that the other may be donated. Unfortunately most of the organs of the body are irreplaceable, so that in the main the doctors have to rely on obtaining replacement organs from those who have died. And the question arises: is it *right* to use the human body in such a way?

Looking at the problem from a very practical standpoint, we can see that very few of us get through life with our bodies intact. A good many of us are without an appendix, most older folks have had their adenoids removed, almost all of us have lost some teeth and more radical surgery accounts for the loss of an entire limb, or part of the stomach or ... well, I needn't add all the gory details. In principle there doesn't seem to be any difference between losing a kidney because of an operation during our lifetime, and *donating* a kidney, to be removed after death.

Some Christians do have a hesitation about this matter of

transplants because there is a feeling that the doctrine of the resurrection is somehow involved. If the feeling is investigated a little further, there is, it seems, a fear that if only part of the body is buried then the resurrection body itself will somehow be incomplete. Looked at in this way the fear is obviously irrational. Since we've all lost some part of the body during our lifetime this would mean that we would all have to face an imperfect resurrection. The real link between the body that is laid to rest in a grave and the spiritual body of the resurrection is *me*, not the ears and bones that were necessary for life on earth. As Professor F. F. Bruce puts it in his book *Answers to Questions*:

> Certainly Paul's conscious self does not go back from being 'with Christ' to be raised from a grave in Rome.

Acting as a donor certainly cannot in any way affect our resurrection.

But there is one potential problem. It is still in the background, but this problem could become very important in the next few years. This is the problem of the transplanting of the brain, or of some part of the brain: neurosurgery. Now we have to be very careful here, because the brain is just as physical as is the kidney. But there is an important difference. Somehow stored in the brain is an unimaginably enormous amount of information collected throughout a lifetime. We don't know exactly how it is stored: probably electrically, although possibly chemistry has something to do with it. We know that this information is stored there and we can sometimes stimulate the brain and make it give up its stored information by means of an electric shock, or by drugs, or even through a sudden shock or blow. The information stored there includes my memories. The features of people I have known are stored away in the brain's picture gallery. The moral teaching I have received is stored there too. And the memories of my sins. Certain impulses seem to be checked, others encouraged by my brain, because of all that I have taught it through the years.

Now the brain isn't *me*. If the brain were *me* then at death

I would myself die, probably gradually as the electrical circuits of the brain gradually broke down. But my brain isn't *me*; it is *mine* in rather a special way.

It would surely be disastrous if attempts were ever made to take spare part surgery out beyond exchanging merely mechanical parts to attempts to transplant the brain, or even part of the brain. The brain would appear to be the principal link between the mechanical me and the essential me, between *me* and *my body*. It would seem to me as dangerous to interfere with the brain at the end of life as it is dangerous to interfere with the genes at the beginning of life. It is, to me, utterly appalling to think of the brains of animals being subjected to experimentation *now*. Experimentation with the human brain would seem to me to be the ultimate assault on God's prerogative.

True enough, we do not need to be too alarmed about this issue as yet, because scientists seem to accept that the time when transplants involving the brain might be considered is very far away indeed. Still, it's not at all a bad thing to get ahead in our thinking, and to be able to say before the issue actually arises: thus far and no further.

Finally, then, to return to the simple issue of organ transplants, it would seem that no new issue is involved. The matter might be easier for us to understand if we could properly appreciate what it means to be blind, and yet to know that the blindness is not really *necessary*. That I *could* see! If only someone would be prepared to donate the corneas of their eyes when they have no further use for them. Or if we could understand the feelings of the thousands who are grateful for the measure of life given to them by the kidney machines, and yet who know that they could return to a normal life if only someone would donate their own kidneys when they have no further use for them. I can only feel that Jesus would encourage us to offer these physical components of the tents we are vacating to those whose own tents could go on functioning a little longer, a little more comfortably, with our help.

Of course, if you are going to take this step then be sure

to contact the appropriate organization (your doctor can give you the details), so that when the time comes your wishes can be met.

Should a Christian minister conduct a funeral for a person who was not a Christian?

Certainly he should. Of course, the minister will be very careful not to say anything during the service which is untrue. But I feel that we should be very much more careful with our comments concerning the spiritual condition of those who have died. For the fact is that we cannot possibly *know* the spiritual condition of another person.

I am reminded again and again of the simplicity of the step of faith that takes a person from death to life by a jingle I once heard:

Between the stirrup and the ground
Mercy I sought and mercy found.

I do believe in last-moment conversions.

We have an example in the New Testament. There were two thieves crucified with Jesus and almost to the end they were both outside the kingdom. Before the great darkness set in, though, one turned to Christ:

'Jesus, remember me when you come into your kingdom.' And [Jesus] said to him, 'Truly, I say to you, today you will be with me in Paradise' (Luke 23:42).

There is always hope, always that last chance. And yet it can never be taken for granted. Again, as someone commented on the two thieves:

One was saved so that no one should ever despair, but only one, so that no one should ever presume.

So, when I come to conduct a funeral service for one who, as far as I know, has not shown evidence of being a Christian, it is not for me to make any pronouncement about his fate.

That is God's prerogative. What I do know is that this person will face God's judgement. My immediate concern must be with those who are left behind. The funeral service may not be able to say much about the life of the one who has gone, but there is much to be said to those left. They need comfort. True, there is nothing that they can do now for the one who has gone. But they have their sorrows. Even the greatest of rascals has often had very real and deep friendships. And beyond that, here is a great opportunity to bring them face to face with reality. All life must eventually face *this* crisis. It is appointed to men to die once. Those who now sit in the chapel grieving for the one who has died must pass the same way.

I agree that this is no time for a lengthy harangue. But surely this *is* the time for the proclamation, clearly and simply, of the love of the God of all comfort, who sent his Son so that whoever believes in him should not perish, but have everlasting life.

4

ON THE OTHER SIDE

What is the second death?

To answer this question we'll need to look at what the Bible says about the first Adam and the last Adam, the first Man and the second Man, the first death and the first resurrection and the second death.

First of all, the first Adam and the last Adam. The Bible is offering us real answers to real problems. For example parents may wonder why their small children are so *naturally* disobedient; why it is that we only need to say to a child, 'Now, don't touch that book,' to find that the book which previously had no particular attraction is now wanted above everything else. Why is it, for a more general example, that revolutions begin with the intention of doing good to everyone, but eventually finish up by producing one more oppressive regime. It *is* so. The Tsarist regime in Russia was an oppressive regime, but who would claim that Stalin's Russia was any the less oppressive? The regime in Ethiopia, under Haile Sellassie *was* an oppressive regime, but the Marxist regime that followed was even more oppressive. And we ask, Why? Politicians ask why.

The Bible answer to all this is usually laughed at, but it's a serious answer for all that: Adam's sin. The utter failure of the first Adam has left us all morally powerless, spiritually bankrupt. With death laid up as the inevitable finale for us all.

Now into that situation comes Christ. Paul gives him two titles: he is the second Man, and he is the last Adam. Between the first Adam and the coming of Christ no one ever saw man as he was intended to be. We did our best, but man was no longer truly man. Jesus was the second Man. He lived just as man had always been meant to live. He ignored the usual concerns for social status. He dedicated himself utterly to the will of his Father for his life. He never did what he wanted to do; hence the amazing statement: 'For Christ did not please himself' (Romans 15:3).

Christ was the second Man, but he was much more than that: he was the last Adam. He undid all that Adam had done. What Adam did Jesus did *not* do. What Adam did not do Jesus *did* do. There is an art form known sometimes as counterchange. It's an interesting technique involving the opposing use of blocks of colour or of patches of black and white. What is black here is white there. The first Adam and the last Adam present us with God's world history in counterchange. Because Jesus is the last Adam, because no other Adam is expected or needed, because of his death for us, Jesus is *not* called the last Man. He is the last Adam, because there will never be any need for another. He is called the second Man because Jesus is the elder brother, the first among many men.

Now the two Adams may be looked on as standing at the head of two families: the redeemed family of the last Adam and the lost family of the first Adam. The entire family of man must face up to the first death. The physical body that so restricts us now has to be shucked off.

But then what? It depends. It depends on the family we belong to. Because after death we still find the same two divisions. All are 'dead', and all have to be raised up, but there are two resurrections, not one. It is God's people who share in the first resurrection and because they have shared in the first resurrection they are spared from the second death.

Long years after the first resurrection has taken place there is a second resurrection. And the resurrected stand before God to be judged. Because they have not taken part in the first resurrection, because they were not of God's family, they share in the second death. They've died once, been raised once, but have yet to 'die' again: 'This is the second death, the lake of fire' (Revelation 20:14).

Now let's have the scriptures from which this particular answer has been put together.

But in fact Christ has been raised from the dead, the first fruits of those who have fallen asleep. For as by a man came death, by a man has come also the resurrection of the dead. For as in Adam all die, so also in Christ shall all be made alive (1 Corinthians 15:20).

Thus it is written, 'The first man Adam became a living being'; the last Adam became a life-giving spirit. But it is not the spiritual which is first but the physical, and then the spiritual. The first man was from the earth, a man of dust; the second man is from heaven (1 Corinthians 15:45–47).

Therefore as sin came into the world through one man and death through sin, and so death spread to all men because all men sinned – sin indeed was in the world before the law was given, but sin is not counted where there is no law. Yet death reigned from Adam to Moses, even over those whose sins were not like the transgression of Adam, who was *a type of the one who was to come*.

But the free gift is not like the trespass. For if many died through one man's trespass, much more have the grace of God and the free gift in the grace of that one man Jesus Christ abounded for many. ... Then as one man's trespass led to condemnation for all men, so one man's act of righteousness leads to acquittal and life for all men. For as by one man's disobedience many were made sinners, so by one man's obedience many will be made righteous (Romans 5:12–19).

And I saw the dead, great and small, standing before the throne, and books were opened. Also another book was opened, which is the book of life. And the dead were judged by what was written in the books, by what they had done. And the sea gave up the dead in it, Death and Hades gave up the dead in them, and all were judged by what they had done. Then Death and Hades were thrown into the lake of fire. This is the second death, the lake of fire; and if anyone's name was not found written in the book of life, he was thrown into the lake of fire (Revelation 20:12–15).

Also I saw the souls of those who had been beheaded for their testimony to Jesus and for the word of God, and who had not worshipped the beast or its image and had not received its mark on their foreheads or their hands. They came to life, and reigned with Christ a thousand years. The rest of the dead did not come to life until the thousand years were ended. This is the first resurrection. Blessed and holy is he who shares in the first resurrection! Over such the second death has no power, but they shall be priests of God and of Christ, and they shall reign with him a thousand years (Revelation 20:4–6).

Are there two resurrections for Christians?

There are certainly two resurrections, but I don't believe that there are two resurrections *for Christians*. The idea of two resurrections comes from Revelation 20:4–6. Now Paul deals with the resurrection in other places, in 1 Thessalonians 4 for example, and there he simply says that 'the dead in Christ will rise first' (verse 16). He is even more explicit in 1 Corinthians 15:51–52:

> Lo! I tell you a mystery. We shall not all sleep, but we shall all be changed, in a moment, in the twinkling of an eye, at the last trumpet.

Notice: we shall *all* be changed, in a moment. So we must understand the passage in Revelation to refer not only to those actually *beheaded* during the final period of tribulation for the church, but to those who died for their faith, no matter how, during that persecution. And we must understand the persecution to refer not only to that final, culminating persecution, but to all such persecutions, and the promise is being made to all believers who faithfully witness even though they are persecuted. One resurrection for all believers. At the last trumpet. One kingdom for us all to share. God's people share *neither* in the second resurrection *nor* in the second death.

Should we really believe in heaven and hell?

Personally I long ago gave up constructing my own theologies and trying to produce my own answers to these really important questions, because my *beliefs* about any subject whatever have no sort of validity at all unless they are based on something which has authority.

If I may say so, that's why I'm writing this book and not simply advising you to read Dr Leslie Weatherhead's book *Life Begins at Death*. In that book he is mostly giving his own opinions on these matters, and refers to the Bible only when what the Bible says happens to fit in with what he believes himself. For example, on page 66 of his book he is asked about judgement and he says, 'I don't think that there is such a thing as a final judgement.' But that's not very helpful, because someone else can come along and say 'Well, I *do* think that there is such a thing as a final judgement.' All we have then got are two opposing statements of two people's beliefs. Which one should I accept? Do I count up years and agree with the older person on the assumption that grey hairs and grey matter go together? Or do I count up degrees and agree with the more academic of the two? Or what?

I do believe in a final judgement *because the Bible describes it*. And the Bible goes on to describe the outcome of the final judgement in terms of heaven and hell. I must say at once that I don't believe that hell is necessarily a *lake* of fire, any more than I believe that heaven is necessarily an enormous city with gigantic walls and streets paved with gold. The Bible is dealing with the spiritual world for which we have no vocabulary. Just as the Bible has to speak of God as though he were like a man with eyes that might close and a nose that can smell incense, simply because we can't imagine a pure spirit, so the Bible has to speak about heaven and hell in terms of streets and gates and fires and pain. Just what the real eternal counterparts of these are, of course, we can't know. Indeed, the Bible says as much about heaven:

> What no eye has seen,
> nor ear heard,
> nor the heart of man conceived,
> what God has prepared for those who love him.
> (1 Corinthians 2:9.)

And another thing. People still cling to the idea that what Jesus taught was a simple gospel of love and that Paul or someone else added the bits about hell and judgement. C. S. Lewis dealt with this back in 1947 when J. B. Phillips' translation of Paul's letters was first published. In the Introduction Lewis wrote:

A most astonishing misconception has long dominated the modern mind on the subject of St Paul. It is to this effect: that Jesus preached a kindly and simple religion (found in the gospels) and that St Paul afterwards corrupted it into a cruel and complicated religion (found in the epistles). This is really quite untenable. All the most terrifying texts come from the mouth of our Lord ...!

So they do. And while I don't subscribe to the view that certain parts of the Bible are more inspired than others (for example, the actual words of Jesus), still it isn't open to those who don't *want* to accept the ideas of judgement, heaven and hell, to blame their fabrication on Paul.

Let's look at the words of Jesus as Mark records them in Mark 9:43–48:

And if your hand causes you to sin, cut it off; it is better for you to enter life maimed than with two hands to go to hell, to the unquenchable fire. And if your foot causes you to sin, cut it off; it is better for you to enter life lame than with two feet to be thrown into hell. And if your eye causes you to sin, pluck it out; it is better for you to enter the kingdom of God with one eye than with two eyes to be thrown into hell, where their worm does not die, and the fire is not quenched.

Now Jesus is using the word *Gehenna*, here, where the English has 'hell'. The word is Hebrew and means 'the valley of Hinnom'. This was the place near to Jerusalem where in Old Testament times human sacrifices had been offered to Molech (2 Chronicles 28:3). Children had actually been burned to death there as sacrifices in Molech worship. And yet Jesus uses this picture of hell, knowing what a powerful and frightening impression this would inevitably give to those who were listening to him.

Notice that in these words of Jesus there is a contrast drawn between the kingdom of God and hell. You enter into the one or the other. There is a choice, there are two possibilities, and the difference between our destiny is made by sin. It is the sin of the hand, the sin of the foot, the sin of the eye that commits a man to hell. It is what we do, where we go, what we stare at that makes the difference. Notice that it is not a question of how well we perform in some kind of theological examination at the final judgement. Sin is the issue.

Now that is all biblical. Whether anything else fits in with this teaching or not is really immaterial. That's what the Book says.

But it *does* fit in. A few months ago my daughter came home from school complaining:

'Daddy, it isn't fair!'

'What isn't fair?'

And then she told me about the examinations they were having at school and the various methods some of the children had worked out to cheat. Some had bits of paper with formulae written on them, some had dates written on their arms, others had a code they used in signalling to their friends in the class room. There was so much cheating going on. And the worst of it all was that no one ever seemed to get caught. So the girls who cheated got more marks than they deserved while the rest stuck to the rules and were penalized for it.

And I had to say:

'Anne, you'll just have to get used to this; life *isn't* fair. These girls don't get caught and they do get more marks than they should. Very often they cheat their way right through life. The only way you'll ever be able to make sense out of life is by remembering that God will one day put it all right. Not in this world. But there *is* another.'

In so many ways life just isn't fair. People have to accept injustice. People have to endure being born into poverty, born with poor health. Children have to take the consequences of broken homes. And it isn't fair. In adult life we find a whole industry in cheating the tax authorities ... and the guilty people get away with it. No, it would be comforting to say that it will catch up with them in the end. But it doesn't seem to. Not in this life, anyway.

But there *is* a judgement:

> And I saw the dead, great and small, standing before the throne, and books were opened. Also another book was opened, which is the book of life. And the dead were judged by what was written in the books, by what they had done (Revelation 20:12).

Am I merely being vindictive when I accept all this? Is there a nasty wish that these cheats will one day get what's coming to them? It could be so, but I notice that John talks of the book of life as well as the record books. The book of life contains the names of all those who have thrown in their lot with Christ. These are the people who have heard the good news and have accepted God's forgiveness. Sin can be forgiven. We don't have to cut off hand and foot and pluck out our eyes in order to escape the hell of which Jesus was speaking. There is forgiveness offered:

> For the wages of sin is death but the free gift of God is eternal life in Christ Jesus our Lord (Romans 6:23).

Is Gehenna the same as hell?

It's rather difficult to know where to begin the answer to this question. I'll either say too much or too little, but on balance I think I'd better risk saying too much.

First of all we have to make a distinction between all those events associated with death *before* Christ's death, and all those events associated with death *after* his death. The whole act of redemption, which involves Christ's death, resurrection and ascension, provides us with a watershed in the theology of death (which actually has its own technical label, *thanatology*). Before these events sin was not dealt with. The Jewish people had offered countless animal sacrifices, but none of them actually dealt with sin: they were regular *reminders* of sin and of the need for some acceptable sacrifice to be made *for* sin (Hebrews

10:1–4 makes this very clear). But *after* these events the account stands paid. On the Old Testament side of the cross, people stand waiting for God to deal with sin. On this, the New Testament side of the cross, God's people stand forgiven, really forgiven.

So then, before Christ's sacrifice was made, God's people, Abraham and David and Isaiah and the rest, *became* God's people just as we do, by faith. But their faith needed to be shown to be reasonable, to correspond to some reality. After all we can have faith in what is actual error. Until fairly recently it was still possible to buy a map of Europe which showed a pass across the Alps which, in fact, didn't exist. In good faith a friend of mine used the map and chose to cross the Alps by that pass. Her faith in the map made no difference whatever to the fact that there was no pass where the map said there was one. Her faith was not justified by events. In a rather similar way, the faith of Abraham and the rest had to be justified by events. They trusted that God *could* find a way of dealing with their sins, and when he *did* find that way their faith was justified. Until that happened they were not freed from their sin.

We can see this argument in Romans 3:24–25. Paul talks of

Christ Jesus, whom God put forward as an expiation by his blood, to be received by faith. This was to show God's righteousness, because in his divine forbearance he had passed over former sins.

Quite unlike the teaching of Islam, which allows God to pass over sin simply out of his compassion, the Bible teaches that God can't do that: it contradicts his own nature, his righteousness. So until Christ dealt with sin God's character remained in question and the Old Testament people of God remained unjustified.

The doctrine of life after death in the Old Testament is not as vague as is sometimes made out. There is always the assumption that the dead are still *there*, somewhere. Man doesn't simply disappear at death. The appearance of necromancy, the practice of consulting the dead, could never have arisen otherwise. And if there were no belief in life after death, Saul would certainly not have bothered with trying to contact the prophet Samuel (1 Samuel 28:8–19) (see the section below: *Will we know one another after death?*). But where *were* the dead? Various words are used in the Old Testament to describe the place, but the most common word is *she'ol*. The word probably means 'the depths'.

Some passages in the Old Testament seem to suggest that Sheol was the place to which the wicked went after death, for example Job 24:19:

> Drought and heat snatch away the snow waters; so does Sheol those who have sinned,

but in fact the Old Testament teaches that there was just one place prepared for all who die:

> Yea, I know that thou wilt bring me to death, and to the house appointed for all living (Job 30:23).

Although most of the Old Testament writers record a horror of *sheol*, Job describes it in more detail than others and with more composure:

> There the wicked cease from troubling,
> and there the weary are at rest.
> There the prisoners are at ease together;
> they hear not the voice of the taskmaster.
> The small and the great are there,
> and the slave is free from his master.
> (Job 3:17–19.)

It appears that Sheol was a place of waiting. A place where the inhabitants were waiting for something to happen, waiting for the next stage. There is clear expectation of an ultimate resurrection:

> Thy dead shall live,
> their bodies shall rise.
> O dwellers in the dust, awake and sing for joy!
> For thy dew is a dew of light
> and on the land of the shades thou wilt let it fall.
> (Isaiah 26:19.)

But between their experience of death and their ultimate resurrection there still lay the death of Christ. When Christ died and rose from among the dead Sheol was transformed. God's people who had 'waited' for the time when their sins could be dealt with now had their faith justified. They were delivered from Sheol and went to be with Christ.

So that's the Old Testament picture.

As we would expect, the New Testament picture far outshines the Old Testament one. First of all, there is no longer any Sheol experience for the people of God, no Hades (as the New Testament calls it) for them. For the Christian looks *back* to Calvary. His faith *is* justified. We *know* that Christ is the Son of God, powerful, because of his resurrection (Romans 1:4). So that when we believe, the past sins are at once dealt with, and *as I sin* the blood of Jesus Christ, God's Son, goes on cleansing from sin (1 John 1:7). Paul understood that to be 'out of the body' was to be 'with Christ' (2 Corinthians 5:8).

So that in the New Testament the believer is with Christ. In Paradise. Let's look at that next.

Death is the gradual weakening of the link that joins the spirit to the body. Of course there will be times when the separation is sudden and violent, for example in a car smash. But more usually dying is the final act of a process of weakening. And when the Christian dies he does not go to sleep. In fact we might almost say that he does the opposite: he suddenly wakes up, home in glory. To quote Weatherhead:

> If you had seen as I have a woman so ill that she couldn't lift her head from the pillow, if you had seen her sit up, her eyes open with tremendous delight, and joy in her face, if you had heard her call the name of a beloved husband who had been dead twenty years, you would find it strangely convincing.

Jesus shared an agonizing death with two thieves. As they shared the experience, one of the thieves appealed to Jesus:

> Jesus, remember me when you come into your kingdom,

and the reply of Jesus was simple and beautiful:

Truly I say to you, today you will be with me in Paradise (Luke 23:39–43).

The word 'Paradise' only occurs six times in the Bible: three times in the Old Testament and three times in the New Testament. In the Old Testament it is translated as 'garden' or 'orchard'. In the New Testament it occurs here, and in 2 Corinthians 12:3 and Revelation 2:7. The word itself is Persian, and originally it referred to a walled garden. When a Persian ruler wanted to reward one of his subjects he would make him a companion of Paradise ... free to walk in the king's garden. And that's what Jesus did for the dying thief:

> Between the twilights of His end
> He made His fellow felon friend;
> With swollen tongue and blinded eyes
> Invited him to Paradise.

Few of us go out of the world like that, but to every one of us God holds out the offer of Paradise: the chance to walk for ever in the garden of the King. When death is seen like that we can all cope with it. Tennyson put it beautifully:

> Sunset and evening star
> and one clear call for me;
> And may there be no moaning of the bar
> when I put out to sea....
> For though from out our bourne of time and place
> the flood may bear me far,
> I hope to see my Pilot face to face,
> when I have crossed the bar.

The various words that are used to describe life after death are all attempting to give us encouragement or warning. The good words like Paradise are a reminder that God has prepared something great for his people, and the bad words, like Gehenna, Sheol, Hades, are a warning: you don't want to find yourself in such a place. The Bible is always struggling to communicate with us in words, when we don't have any words that really fit heaven or hell.

And that brings us to the idea of *heaven*. Let's define that a little more carefully as the final home of the people of God. We need a definition like that because the Bible speaks of more than one heaven. In Genesis 1:1 we read that God created the *heavens* and the earth, so right from the beginning there was more than one. Then in Revelation 21:1 we find a new heaven:

> Then I saw a new heaven and a new earth; for the first heaven and the first earth had passed away.

So we go from one end of the Bible to the other and find that it is talking about heaven at both ends. And to make things even more complicated Paul talks about being caught up in some kind of visionary experience into the *third* heaven (2 Corinthians 12:2).

Just as Sheol or Hades (Sheol is Hebrew, Hades is Greek) is still, even now, the waiting place for those who have died rejecting God, and there they 'await' their special judgement at the end of history, so Christians await their own final judgement and final home. But we have to be very careful here. First, the Christian is not judged to determine whether or not he is good enough to be allowed into heaven. That's all settled. He isn't good enough, but since Christ has himself taken all the sin of the Christian nothing is left for the Christian to carry. So judgement is *not* to decide whether or not we get to heaven. Secondly, the Christian is not separated from God as he awaits the judgement. As we have already seen, to be absent from the body is to be present with the Lord. And thirdly, the purpose of the judgement is reward, not punishment.

On this last issue let's note what Paul says about rewards in his letter to Corinth:

> each man's work will become manifest; for the Day will disclose it, because it will be revealed with fire, and the fire will test what sort of work each one has done. If the work which any man has built on the foundation survives, he will receive a reward. If any man's work is burned up, he will suffer loss, though he himself will be saved, but only as through fire (1 Corinthians 3:13–15).

Notice here that Paul speaks of *rewards* and of *loss*, but not of *punishment*. The consequences even of our laziness and prayerlessness have all been borne by Christ, so there is no question of our being punished for them as well. But the Bible does make it clear that we have to answer for the way in which we have used our lives. Where they have been well used, the testing fire will show it, and God will reward the Christian. On the other hand, where the life has been self-centred, undisciplined, loveless, thoughtless, characterized by greed or pride or jealousy, the fire will show it. It will all be destroyed, and I suppose that it is conceivable that some Christians could come through this judgement with *nothing* but salvation.

And it's from there on that we can talk about heaven, when those who have died in Christ have been transformed and united with the similarly transformed host still alive at Christ's return; when together they have been judged and appropriately rewarded, and so move together into the new heaven.

It's easy to see why this judgement has to precede the entry into the new heaven:

> And I saw no temple in the city, for its temple is the Lord God the Almighty and the Lamb. And the city has no need of sun or moon to shine upon it, for the glory of God is its light, and its lamp is the Lamb. By its light shall the nations walk; and the kings of the earth shall bring their glory into it, and its gates shall never be shut by day – and there shall be no night there; they shall bring into it the glory and the honour of the nations. *But nothing unclean shall enter it*, nor anyone who practises abomination or falsehood, but only those who are written in the Lamb's book of life (Revelation 21:22–27).

So, then, we have: Sheol or Hades, the waiting place of the unbelieving dead, waiting judgement and hell, Paradise and the presence of God for the believers as they await judgement and reward, and their new home in heaven. (See also the section below: *Why does the creed say that Jesus 'descended into hell'?*)

All of this must seem very simplistic, even naïve, to the philosopher, the intellectual – Sheol or Hades, paradise, heaven and hell. Surely we don't have to believe all that. My answer is simple. In some matters it's enough to make a good guess, and if you're wrong it may not matter too much. Train time-tables are an example. I'm not quite sure when the next train leaves, but I *think* that there's one at about six-thirty. And if I'm wrong, well, there'll be one along fairly soon, and not too much harm done. But with some things we have to *know*. If we *can* know, that is. But no one is able to tell us about life after death, because we don't have return tickets beyond the grave. Only God can tell us. And I believe that he has, through the Bible. What is said there makes sense to me. I think that I see more and more clearly the principles lying behind what God describes. And at any rate, no one has come up with a clearer explanation. No one has a more authoritative explanation. And I need to *know*:

> But ah! to know not while with friends I sit,
> and while the purple joy is passed about,
> whether 'tis ampler day, divinelier lit
> or homeless night without.

> And whether, stepping forth, my soul shall see
> new prospects, or fall sheer – a blinded thing:
> There is, O grave, thy hourly victory,
> and there, O death, thy sting.
>
> William Watson

It's all there in the Book. And it just doesn't seem to me logical, scholarly or even honest, to do what so many writers on death have done, to pick out the bits of the Bible they do approve of, and to throw out the bits they don't approve of. There *is* a systematic picture of life after death given in the Bible, and the attempt to improve on it simply destroys the harmony of the whole. And it substitutes a quite unsatisfactory patchwork of myth and imagination. I learned a good many years ago to stay with the Book.

Can you explain David's words when the son born to him and Bathsheba died?

2 Samuel chapters 11 and 12: most of us know the story of David and Bathsheba. It's ironic when we notice how the whole history begins:

> In the spring of the year, the time when kings go forth to battle, David sent Joab and his servants with him, and all Israel, and they ravaged the Ammonites and besieged Rabbah. But David remained at Jerusalem.
> It happened late one afternoon, when David arose from his couch ... (11:1–2).

At the time when the kings went to war, David went to bed.

David saw Bathsheba bathing – possibly accidentally, more probably deliberately exposed to his lustful eyes. He took her and when she became pregnant he arranged to have her husband killed by the defendants of Rabbah. And then he married her. But David's cynical attempt to regularize fornication and murder by marriage struck at the character of God. For the kings of Judah reigned as God's representatives. What had happened couldn't be hushed up. Everybody must have known just what had happened, and probably measured against the usual behaviour of kings there was nothing particularly striking about what David did. But David's behaviour reflected on the God who had chosen him: *this* was the man after God's own heart!

The baby was taken ill, and at the end of a week it was dead. Throughout the week David, now aware of his sin, had prayed and fasted in the hope that maybe, somehow, God's judgement could be turned away. But the baby died. And when he died David said, simply,

> Can I bring him back again? I shall go to him, but he will not return to me (2 Samuel 12:23).

Now two things need to be said about this event. The first comment might, perhaps, be a help to anyone who has lost a child. We think that death is the very worst thing that can happen to us. It may seem very hard to struggle through to a realization that we are wrong. That is *not* the Christian view of death. Life itself is by no means easy. There is inevitable heartache, struggle, illness, loss, the feeling of inadequacy and at the end of it all death. To go to God, back to the God who made us, should surely be a very wonderful thing.

The Venerable Bede recorded the story of the coming of the good news to Northumbria in the north of England. King Edwin ruled at the time, and he was in doubt as to whether he should allow this new teaching to be spread about in his lands, or whether he should stop it at once. As he thought it over, he called in his counsellors, and it was one of them who said:

> The present life of man on earth, O king, seems to me, in comparison with that time which is unknown to us, like the swift flight of a sparrow. It is as though you were seated in your castle with your Ealdormen and thegns, in winter. Within, the fire blazes, and in the midst the hall is warmed, but without the wintry storms of rain or snow rage, the sparrow, flying in at one door and immediately out at another. Whilst he is within he is safe from the tempest, but after a short space of fair weather he immediately vanishes out of your sight, passing *from* winter back into winter again. So this life of man appears for a little while, but of what is to follow, or what went before we know nothing at all. If, therefore, this new teaching tells us something more certain, it seems justly to deserve being followed.

King Edwin followed the advice. In 627 he was baptized.

But still, the old man's ideas were all wrong. He had the picture quite the wrong way round. In fact the storm is *in the castle*! We sit, huddled around the fire, muffled against the storms of life, with the bitter winds raging about us, little knowing that outside, in the greater world, the sun is shining. And it's back into *that* world that the little life has gone.

The second comment concerns that idea of a 'little life'. We believe that man is singly infinite, infinite in one direction only. He is created, and having been created he goes on living to all eternity future. God is doubly infinite. He is uncreated, and his being reaches back into all eternity past and on into all eternity future. As Jesus put it of his own eternal character:

Before Abraham *was*, I *am* (John 8:58).

So every baby that is born is the physical, viewable, touchable, recognizable vehicle of an eternal soul. The soul is spiritual, and has spiritual powers. Being spiritual it doesn't get older, because it relates directly to God's spiritual world, the real world, where there is no time. The created soul seems to be created so that God might share with it his love.

That's all rather heavy going, so let me pause and recap. Each baby represents an eternal soul, an eternal spiritual being. A being that doesn't get *old*. The soul isn't a baby. The soul isn't 'a little life'.

God created a perfect soul for the body so laboriously formed in the womb of the mother. The body would need to grow, to be trained, to be disciplined, and the mind would need to be taught. It would seem that the body is the workshop of the soul. The soul of man fashions the body, the mind, the will, until at last it leaves the body, and has to answer to God for the task it has done. When the soul is released from its task it is free to return to God who made it. Death itself is not cruel. The cruelty is for us, left here in the winter of life, while the soul of the child returns to the summer of God's eternity.

So that was what happened to the soul of the baby born to David and Bathsheba: it returned to God who created it. But it was not a *baby* soul. Eventually the soul of David also returned to God who had created it. But David's soul was not an *aged* soul. At the end of his life David was a rather pathetic, chewed up old man who couldn't seem to keep warm (1 Kings 1:1), but that shouldn't make us think of his *soul* as being pathetic and shrivelled. The idea of *age* simply doesn't apply to the spiritual side of man.

Nor should we think of the soul of the baby as *small*, any more than we should think of David's soul as *big*. Once again these spatial terms simply don't apply to the soul.

Now I don't imagine for one moment that such thoughts

were in David's mind when he used the words we are discussing here: 'I shall go to him, but he will not return to me.' Without wondering how it could be, David was expressing his faith that life continues beyond death, that both his own life and the life of the baby would continue, and that they would somehow be related to one another in the next world as they were related to one another in this world.

His words were precisely *not* words of despair. David did *not* respond: 'It's all over for the baby and one day it will be all over for me too.' His was a robust faith that reached out beyond death: 'There's no need to sorrow for the child. Safe home, out of the storm. I can't call him back here. But still, we shall meet again. We shall know one another. I shall know him, not as a screwed up, helpless little scrap of humanity, but the full soul that was my son. And he'll know me, not as the lustful, assertive father who brought him into the world, nor as the old man who tottered into death, but as the real me, the essential me that has always been struggling against the confines of my body: the butterfly trying to escape from the confining chrysalis that will one day split to release me. This is not the end. We shall meet again.'

Will we know one another after death?

Yes. Now, we are thinking about two worlds, the present world where we are severely limited by our bodies and minds, and the world we shall one day enter, the world of freedom from all limitations. Surely we are going to know *more* then than we know now? Surely the present limitations will all give way to perfect knowledge. Or as George MacDonald put it, rather more bluntly:

Shall we be greater fools in Paradise than we are here?

But let's look at the biblical evidence. First of all we look into the Old Testament and the account of the return to this world of the prophet Samuel. At the end of his life, Saul found himself in rebellion against God, rebelled against by his own people and attacked by the Philistines. Unable to get any kind of picture of the future he determined to resort to necromancy: consultation with the dead. This is a very ancient practice, still found today in spiritism, making use of a 'control' or 'familiar spirit' as the Old Testament expresses it. The control is the spirit of someone who has died and for some reason has been able to establish contact with the living. The control obviously has certain knowledge concerning the afterlife and may be able to transmit some of that illicit information to the medium.

The practice itself is condemned in the Old Testament:

> There shall not be found among you any one who burns his son or his daughter as an offering, any one who practices divination, a soothsayer, or an augur, or a sorcerer, or a charmer, or a medium, or a wizard, or a necromancer (Deuteronomy 18:10–11).

Now although Saul had himself banned necromancers from his kingdom, some remained, and he determined to consult the woman who practised at Endor, near Mount Tabor. There is no doubt at all that the woman had access to the dead in Sheol, and that they were able to give her knowledge which she did not herself possess. An immediate example occurs in the account we have of this incident in 1 Samuel 28. When Saul comes to her, in disguise, she does not recognize her visitor. But as soon as Samuel is called up from Sheol she is made aware of Saul's identity (verse 12):

> When the woman saw *Samuel*, she cried out with a loud voice; and the woman said to Saul, 'Why have you deceived me? You are Saul.'

The reality of the communication between this woman and the dead Samuel is not in doubt. But it is interesting to notice that Saul *knows* Samuel. We are told that the woman *saw* Samuel, appearing to her as 'an old man ... wrapped in a robe'. But although we read that Saul *knew* that it was Samuel we are not told that Saul ever *saw* the apparition. He *knew* who it was, without having to *see* who it was. There is a suggestion here that the spiritual world may manifest itself to the physical world, and that somehow it is able to communicate with the physical world non-verbally, without using speech. Samuel communicated *Saul's* identity to the medium, and *his own* identity to Saul.

In the New Testament we have a fascinating account of the in-breaking of eternity upon time in the story of the transfiguration of Christ. When Jesus took his three closest followers, Peter, John and James, up a mountain (probably Mount Hermon) for prayer, he himself was suddenly transformed, and so were his clothes. From being an apparently ordinary person he became somehow different: still recognizably Jesus and yet a glorified Jesus: 'they saw his glory' (Luke 9:32). From being ordinary clothes, stained with the inevitable dust from the climb up the mountain, they began to gleam with a dazzling whiteness. Along with these phenomena directly affecting the person of the Lord there was the unheralded and unexplained appearance of two figures with Jesus. The word 'glory' is associated with them, too: they 'appeared in glory' (verse 31).

As all this was happening, the three followers of Jesus were asleep. But when they awoke, and saw the three glorious figures, they knew them all:

> Peter said to Jesus, 'Master, it is well that we are here; let us make three booths, one for you and one for Moses and one for Elijah' – not knowing what he said (Luke 9:33).

That's interesting: *not knowing what he said.* He blurted out this knowledge of his, not knowing that he knew! There's no indication in the accounts we have in Matthew 17:1–8; Mark 9:2–8; Luke 9:28–36 or the reference in 2 Peter 1:16–18 that anyone had to *tell* Peter who these visitors were. In the Old Testament reference to Saul and Samuel, Saul had known Samuel during his lifetime, so that it might be argued that Saul recognized Samuel in a natural way, but in the appearance of Moses and Elijah no such prior acquaintance existed. All that I'm saying is that the dead do seem to return under certain circumstances, that they are still the same individuals and that they are recognizable, possibly because they are able to make themselves known directly, rather than merely verbally.

Next, there's the insight given by Jesus into life after death, more specifically into life after death for two particular individuals, a rich man and Lazarus. The Latin *dives* ('rich man') has been turned into a proper name; the Bible account in Luke 16:19–31 does not give him a name. Here are two men, the one rich and the other poor. We do *not* read that the poor man ate the scraps from the rich man's table; we *are* told that he would have liked to eat the scraps from the rich man's table. The story turns on the character of the rich man who, with more than enough to eat each day, and with a beggar at hand whom he might easily have cared for, thought only of himself. Both died. The body of the rich man was buried, no doubt with suitable mourning. What happened to the emaciated body of the poor man we are not told.

After death there is a separation. The one suffers, the other is comforted. In Sheol the rich man, now beggared, looks up and sees Lazarus. No doubt he had seen Lazarus often enough, lying at his gate, so that it is not particularly surprising that he recognizes him; but *he also recognizes Abraham.* He correctly identifies a man he had never seen.

Finally, we have the evidence of the resurrection of Jesus. We notice that Jesus had the power both to reveal himself to his followers and to conceal himself from them. In John 20 we find Mary in tears, near the tomb where Jesus had been buried. He is risen, the tomb is empty, but she doesn't yet believe. Even conversation with angels doesn't help, and then:

> ... she turned around and saw Jesus standing, but she did not know that it was Jesus (verse 14).

It was only when Jesus spoke her name that she knew him.

Again, we have the account of the walk to Emmaus. Cleopas and another of Christ's disciples were walking to Emmaus, and then:

> Jesus himself drew near and went with them. But their eyes were kept from recognizing him (Luke 24:15–16).

It's not until the walk is over, and Jesus has taken the bread into his own hands and spoken the blessing, that

> their eyes were opened, and they recognized him; and he vanished out of their sight (Luke 24:31).

The ten knew him when he appeared to them in the upper room. So did Thomas, a week later. At the sea of Tiberias, the Lake of Galilee, John, the disciple whom Jesus loved (why *will* the scholars try to make it out to be anyone *except* John?), recognized the Lord standing by the lakeside (John 21:7). Once again we see that there was a new power, a new facility in the greater life we shall one day share: the power to make ourselves known.

This question of whether or not we shall know one another is an important question, and while we don't have a direct answer to it we do have enough in Scripture to be able to construct a biblical answer. The answer is, yes, we shall know one another after death. More than that, we'll 'recognize' people we have never known before. Our powers there are going to be greater than they are here, not less.

Will we have bodies similar to the ones we have now?

The bodies we shall have will certainly be better than those we now have, but before I go on to look at the new body promised to us, perhaps I could comment on the bodies we now have. Our present bodies, designed by God, part of his creation, are not *vile* bodies as the old Authorized Version suggested in its translation of Philippians 3:21.

> For our conversation is in heaven; from whence also we look for the Saviour, the Lord Jesus Christ: Who shall change our vile body, that it may be fashioned like unto his glorious body ...

The original Greek word here translated 'vile' simply means 'humble'. It is the same word as the one used by Mary in the Magnificat:

He has put down the mighty from their thrones, and exalted those *of low degree* (Luke 1:52).

Our bodies are not vile, but they are weak. The New English Bible describes this human body as 'the body belonging to our humble state'. God created it, and it does form part of the fallen universe, but still it's a marvel, a wonder of creation, weak and humble, but not 'vile'.

Still, the human body *is* weak, and all through our lives we are aware of its weakness, as germs try to break through its defences and as age gradually wears it down. Despite the present humiliating weakness of the body, however, it is interesting to notice that the Bible view is opposed to the concept of a disembodied spirit. This may in part explain the Lukan account of the Gadarene or Gerasene pigs. They were, apparently, being pastured near to Galilee when Jesus was dealing with the man who had been possessed by an assortment of demons. Jesus commanded the demons to come out of the man (Luke 8:29), but while they could not resist his authority they begged for some kind of locus, a *place* to be located, even if it should be the body of a pig. The demons appeared to have a real fear of being without a body, of being spatially unlocated.

It is Luke, also, who records Jesus' words concerning the behaviour of evil spirits:

> When the unclean spirit has gone out of a man he passes through waterless places seeking rest; and finding none he says, 'I will return to my house from which I came' (Luke 11:24).

The spirit, apparently, finds no rest in mere bodiless wandering, but actively seeks some kind of physical location. It is particularly interesting, here, to notice the mention of the spirit wandering in *waterless places*, since in my experience of spirit possession I have found that the spirits tend to be territorially limited, and invariably the physical boundary which limits them is a stream or river, or perhaps a spring. Within the area delimited the spirit is forced to find a body which it can possess.

Paul expresses this general abhorrence of the spirit of the disembodied state; the Good News Bible expresses it well:

And now we sigh, so great is our desire that our home which comes from heaven should be put on over us; by being clothed with it we shall not be found *without a body*. While we live in this earthly tent, we groan with a feeling of oppression; it is not that we want to get rid of our earthly body, but that we want to have the heavenly one put on over us, so that what is mortal will be transformed by life (2 Corinthians 5:2–4).

A picture begins to emerge here of the present human body being covered, concealed, replaced, by a new 'heavenly' body. This is, apparently, a change which follows death, and is intended to avoid the disembodying of the spirit. The new body is to be given as the old body is shed. We must be careful not to press this temporal, time-orientated thinking on a situation which in fact refers to life beyond time. After all the new body is given to us at Christ's return, at the resurrection, and we have to 'wait' until then for it. But, as we have already seen, words like 'before', 'after' and 'until' don't really apply to the eternal world to which we go when we leave this one.

We will have a new body after death. The Bible rejects the concept of disembodied spirits. But what is the new body like? We have seen that the spirit has the power to make its identity known, apparently even to those who were unknown to the spirit during its time on earth. And the spirit could manifest itself so that it could be visually seen and recognized. So the new body obviously has some kind of direct relationship to the old material body. The relationship is difficult to describe precisely, but Paul illustrates the relationship quite clearly in 1 Corinthians 15:35–44:

But some one will ask, 'How are the dead raised? With what kind of body do they come?' You foolish man! What you sow does not come to life unless it dies. And what you sow is not the body which is to be, but a bare kernel, perhaps of wheat or of some other grain. But God gives it a body as he has chosen, and to each kind of seed its own body.... What is sown is perishable, what is raised is imperishable. It is sown in dishonour, it is raised in glory. It is sown in weakness, it is raised in power. It is sown a physical body, it is raised a spiritual body.

The illustration used by Paul is a very helpful one: the illustration of seed and plant. I'm not a particularly good gardener, but in Ethiopia I grew a lot of eucalyptus trees from seed. The seed is a tiny black speck, but now, just outside Addis Ababa, or two hundred miles to the south where I lived for a couple of years, you can see today what grew from those tiny black seeds. Now what grew was *not* a series of enormous black spheres, but fine, sweeping trees, not black, but brown and green and silver in the highland winds. Not ugly, but beautiful. Not sullenly immobile but vibrantly alive, growing.

That is Paul's inspired illustration of the resurrection body. When I want carrots it's not carrots that I plant but tiny flaky, light-coloured seeds. When I want eucalyptus trees to grow I don't plant a eucalyptus tree but a shrivelled black seed. But there *is* a relationship between what is sown and what grows. The whole tree is somehow encapsulated in the shrivelled black seed. There is a relationship between the spiritual body that I will have and the physical body that I now possess.

In Philippians 3:21 Paul gives a further hint concerning the nature of the resurrection body. He speaks of Christ who will

> change our lowly body to be like his glorious body, by the power which enables him even to subject all things to himself.

This further glimpse is a reminder that God's purpose is simply that the whole universe should glorify Christ: every one will bow to him, every one will confess that he is Lord. Everything else in history is subordinated to this over-riding concern, that Christ should be pre-eminent. So it is right that our spiritual bodies will be like his spiritual body: sharing in its glory and its power.

It is a simple fact that I write upon my body the history of my life. It is scarred on the hand because once I had a childish disagreement with my twin brother over who should wash up the carving knife. It is scarred on the other hand because of an accident in the research laboratory where I worked. Miscellaneous other scars mark the efforts of various doctors to put right the workings of some of my plumbing. My eyes tend to be narrowed as a result of many hours of mule-riding in the blazing sun of Ethiopia. My body is a visual history of my life. Invisibly preserved within is my brain, in the complex circuits of which are locked away most of what I have ever said or done. All of that will one day be consigned to the dust. And out of it will come, somehow, a resurrected, glorious body, different from it but related to it and at the same time related to Christ's glorious body; somehow recognizably *me*.

5

THE DEATH OF CHRIST

What was the cause of Christ's death?

The death of Christ was a supernatural, not a natural event. No one killed him, no one executed him, no one took his life from him:

> For this reason the Father loves me, because I lay down my life, that I may take it again. No one takes it from me, but I lay it down of my own accord. I have power to lay it down, and I have power to take it again (John 10:17–18).

We know that the death of Christ only six hours after he was nailed to the cross was unexpected. There were three crucified together, at the same time. Of those three one laid down his life, while two had life taken from them. We know that Jesus' death was unexpected by Pilate:

> ... as evening approached, Joseph of Arimathea, a prominent member of the Council, who was himself waiting for the kingdom of God, went boldly to Pilate and asked for Jesus' body. Pilate was surprised to hear that he was already dead. Summoning the centurion, he asked him if Jesus had already died. When he learned from the centurion that it was so, he gave the body to Joseph (Mark 15:42–5, New International Version).

The reason for Pilate's surprise is obvious: normally those who were crucified lingered on for *days* before dying. This was the reason for the soldiers' action in hastening the deaths of the other two who were crucified with Jesus. The bodies could not be left on the crosses through the Passover, but in the normal course of events these men would not die before the end of the day.

There have been several theories to explain the death of Jesus, all produced by medical people, and all missing the real point: this was not a man dying in the usual way, but the Son of God laying down his life for the sin of the world. Medical people point to the experiences of Jesus as contributing to his death. He was hungry and thirsty: he had nothing to eat or drink after the Passover meal the preceding evening. He had spent a long time in the agony of prayer in Gethsemane. He had been beaten by the soldiers. He had lost blood from the scourging, probably from the crown of thorns, and certainly from the wounds produced by the actual crucifixion. He was exposed to the heat of the eastern sun, although for three hours that sun was covered over, diminishing his suffering from this cause. The crucifixion itself was horrific. The victim was fastened to the cross while it was still on the ground, with nails through hands and feet. Only recently the remains of just such a victim were discovered, setting at rest the argument of some that those who were crucified were tied to the cross, not nailed to it. In this recently discovered case the nail which had transfixed the ankles was still there. When the cross was set up vertically the sufferer would be exposed to the glare of the sun, to the tearing pain of the nail wounds, to thirst and to the mockery of the crowds. In addition, because of the unnatural posture, there would be real difficulty in breathing.

But what was the actual cause of Jesus' death? Some doctors have suggested that he died from a ruptured heart. It is out of this idea that the popular notion of his dying of a 'broken heart' has arisen. By a ruptured heart is simply meant a break in the walls between the chambers of the heart which would make it impossible for the heart to continue to circulate the blood. But we know that such a rupture, while now well attested, is a consequence of disease, not of shock, and there is no evidence whatever to suggest that Jesus suffered, for example, from arteriosclerosis.

A second suggestion, which similarly directs attention to the heart, is that Jesus died from an embolism, a blood clot which then blocked a vital artery. But again there is no evidence to suggest that Jesus had any disease which might produce such a blood clot, and as far as is known neither blood clot nor heart rupture can be produced by mental anguish, however great.

Thirdly there is the suggestion that Jesus died of asphyxia. We have already commented on the fact that crucifixion, in which the arms are stretched out while the body hangs down, makes breathing difficult. But while it certainly makes breathing difficult we must remember that all who were crucified suffered in this same way, and yet most still lived on for more than a day. Why should others be able to breathe when Jesus could not? And again, if Jesus died of asphyxia how could he, just before he died, 'cry out with a loud voice' (Mark 15:34)? We would expect a whisper rather than a shout.

Perhaps it is natural to expect medical people to look for a medical reason to explain the death of Christ, but it is wrong, precisely because it is natural. Christ's death was not natural, but supernatural.

The Bible is, in fact, very careful in describing the moment of Christ's death:

And Jesus cried again with a loud voice and yielded up his spirit (Matthew 27:50).

And Jesus uttered a loud cry and breathed his last (Mark 15:37).

Then Jesus, crying with a loud voice, said, 'Father, into Thy hands I commit my spirit!' And having said this he breathed his last (Luke 23:46).

When Jesus had received the vinegar he said, 'It is finished'; and he bowed his head and gave up his spirit (John 19:30).

Not one of these writers is content to say, simply, 'Jesus died'.

Now the Bible is inspired. The four evangelists did not have to sit down to work out how they were to phrase these matters. As they wrote so the Holy Spirit directed them. And it is vital to notice not only what the writers do say, but also what they do not say. Here, the writers do not say that Jesus died, although at other points in the account we are told this very plainly. The point being made is that no one killed Jesus. He was not, himself, subject to death. He gave up his life. He offered himself by the eternal Spirit (Hebrews 9:14) as a sacrifice to God the Father.

The rest of us are not able to determine the moment of death except by suicide. I may shoot myself, poison myself or hang myself, but I cannot merely dismiss my spirit. I cannot decide, 'I will die now.' In fact I well remember a friend of mine who was a Professor at Addis Ababa University, and he was very seriously ill in hospital. The doctors came to him and told him that he was dying. As he told the story, this was what happened:

'I am sorry to have to tell you that we cannot do anything for you. You are dying.'

Pause, while my friend took this rather stark announcement in. Then: 'I am dying? I won't recover?'

'No.'

Pause again, then:

'Well, what am I supposed to do?'

The doctors were rather taken aback by this matter of fact approach:

'Er ... well, perhaps turn on your side and relax yourself.'

Calmly he did as they suggested, and lay there quietly for a few minutes and then turned back again:

'I can't seem to do it!'

He couldn't just die.

But Jesus could, and did.

We should be careful when we talk about the death of Jesus. We sometimes hear questions about who killed him. Was it the Jews, who accused him? Was it the Romans who crucified him? No, nor was it me, even though it was for me that Jesus went to the cross. No one took his life from him: he laid it down, himself.

Why do Muslims say that Jesus did not die on the cross?

Probably many people have had this rather shattering experience of a visit from Muslims who say that Jesus did not die on the cross. The reason for this particular attack on the cross is that if only the cross can be taken away as the place where Christ died, a sacrifice for sin for ever, then Christianity is finished. In fact, Islam even has a book called *Deliverance from the Cross* all devoted to the one task of 'proving' that Jesus did not die on the cross.

Actually there are two different lines of teaching among the Muslims concerning the cross. Traditionally the Muslims have taught that Jesus was not crucified at all. Instead someone else was crucified: some suggest Judas Iscariot. Jesus was safely carried away by angels to heaven and so was never crucified. More recently we have had the *Ahmadiyya* Muslims, named after their founder who claimed to be the Messiah of Judaism, the Prophet of Islam, an incarnation of the Hindu deity Krishna and the Light of the World. The Ahmadiyya teach that Jesus *was* crucified but he did not die on the cross. Instead he only appeared to die, but Nicodemus (who becomes, without any evidence at all, a skilled doctor) and Joseph revived him in the cool of the tomb. After his recovery Jesus is supposed to have gone off to India and to have died in Kashmir. There is no explanation as to why he should have abandoned his followers and gone to India, nor any explanation as to why the apostles preached the resurrection.

Both of these teachings come from one rather obscure verse of the Qur'an. According to 'Women' (that is Sura 4 of the Qur'an), verse 154, Allah has 'sealed up' the Jews ...

... for their saying, 'Verily we have slain the Messiah,
Jesus the son of Mary, an Apostle of God.'
Yet they slew him not
and they crucified him not.
but *they had only his likeness*.
And they who differed about him were in doubt concerning him:

No sure knowledge had they about him,
but followed only an opinion,
and they did not really slay him,
but God took him up to Himself.

What is clear in this passage is the insistence that Jesus was not killed by the Jews. Notice that this passage does not actually say that Jesus did not die: it does say that the Jews did not slay him.

Actually the words of the Qur'an are not too easily translated at this point. The vital words 'they had only his likeness' (Rodwell's translation) are translated 'he was counterfeited for them' by Bell, 'it appeared to them as such' by Massignon and 'only a likeness of that was shown them' by Arberry. An entirely different translation is given by Sir Muhammad Zafrullah Khan, an Ahmadiyya Muslim, who translates: 'the semblance of death was created for them'.

Now out of this mixture three interpretations have come. Traditionally Muslims have believed that Jesus was not crucified at all. Instead God concealed Jesus, and made the soldiers and the disciples confused, so that all saw Judas Iscariot as though he were Jesus. It was Judas who was crucified. This idea is most clearly seen in a book that the Muslim may quote to you, the Gospel of Barnabas. This is a Muslim forgery from the sixteenth century and tells the whole story of the crucifixion from the standpoint of the Qur'an.

The problem with this interpretation is, of course, that it flies in the face of the evidence. It leaves unexplained the story of the empty tomb, and contradicts the account of the suicide of Judas. True enough these problems are easily dealt with, since according to Islam where the Bible differs from the Qur'an it is because Jews and Christians have changed the Bible. This means that while the Muslim can pick out the bits of the Bible he wants to use, we can never use the bits that we want to use. But the Muslim fabrication really won't do. The death of Christ is one of the best attested facts in all history!

So there is a second line of interpretation. Some Muslims realize that the death of Christ on the cross cannot be denied.

So they come back to my answer to the previous question, namely that the Jews did not kill Jesus, even though they thought they killed him. They couldn't kill Jesus: he laid down his own life. This interpretation follows Massignon's translation of Sura 4, verse 154: 'it appeared to them as such' but in fact '*they* slew him not'.

The third line of interpretation is that of the Ahmadiyya Muslims who say that Jesus was crucified, but did not die on the cross. The sponge filled with sour wine 'suffocated' Jesus (although how he then cried out with a loud voice we are not told), he appeared to die (although how the soldiers, and especially the centurion who had to verify his death, were deceived we are not told), was hurriedly taken down from the cross and carried to the tomb where he was anointed with spices (although why he was anointed with them if they knew he was not dead we are not told). This, along with the expert ministry of Nicodemus (who becomes an 'expert physician', for which there is no evidence whatever) brought him back to life.

This last approach simply is a pack of cards. The book *Deliverance from the Cross* is full of confident statements, such as: 'There can be no doubt that Joseph and Nicodemus must have continued to minister unto Jesus in the strong hope of reviving him;' 'nothing whatever had happened from which an inference of death could reasonably be drawn;' 'the fact that the heart of Jesus was beating after his body was removed from the cross has been proved beyond doubt and cannot be contradicted.' It *can* be contradicted:

being found in human form he humbled himself and became obedient *unto death*, even death on a cross (Philippians 2:8).

When they came to Jesus and saw that he was *already dead*, they did not break his legs (John 19:33).

Joseph of Arimathea ... went to Pilate, and asked for the body of Jesus. And Pilate wondered if he were already dead; and summoning the centurion, he asked him whether he was already dead. And when he learned from the centurion that *he was dead*, he granted the body to Joseph (Mark 15:43–45).

If Muslim missionaries use such dogmatic phrases as 'there can be no doubt' and 'obviously' it is because there is a great deal of doubt and it is not obvious at all.

It *is* Muslim teaching that Jesus did not die on the cross. This is only one of many errors in the Qur'an. But it simply will not do to have Muhammad, writing some six hundred years after the death and resurrection of Jesus, re-writing the gospel story. What is tragic is that the Muslim writers are able to quote so-called Christian writers, Anglican 'theologians', who deny the deity of Christ and refer to the resurrection as a myth. I must say that I fail to understand why such 'theologians' remain in the Anglican church. Even more I fail to understand why they are *allowed* to remain. I thank God that the Ethiopian church to which I belonged would have known better than to allow such people to stay.

Can you explain the prophecy that Jesus would be 'three days and three nights' in the heart of the earth?

This particular form of the prophecy occurs only in Matthew 12:40,

> For as Jonah was three days and three nights in the belly of the whale, so will the Son of man be three days and three nights in the heart of the earth.

The most straightforward answer to this question was given by Edersheim in his magnificent book, *The Life and Times of Jesus the Messiah*. There he points out that the mention of any day carries with it the associated night. Similarly the mention of a night would indicate the inclusion of its related day. It does not seem possible, in spite of all manner of attempts to do so, to bring about any change in the traditional way of placing the events of the crucifixion. So here is the sequence:

> Friday: Jesus is crucified and dies. But the *day*, the twenty-four hours of Friday, includes what we would call Thursday night and Friday morning. *One night and one day.*

Saturday: Jesus rests in the tomb; his body still, his ministry
continuing. Saturday's twenty-four hours would include Saturday night and Sunday morning. *One night and one day.*

Sunday: Jesus rises from the dead. This is the first day of the week,
and its twenty-four hours would include Sunday evening and
Monday morning. *One day and one night.*

Thus the three days and three nights actually spread from
Thursday night to Sunday night. Of course Jesus was not
actually in the grave all that time, any more than Jonah was
in the whale for three sequences of twenty-four hours. The
'three days and three nights' were understood in the same way
by the Jews of Jonah's day and by the Jews of Jesus' day. In
fact the phrase is rather like the French word for a week, a
huit-jour, literally '*eight* days'. Actually in Ethiopia they speak
a Semitic language, rather like Hebrew, and we too spoke of
a *sammint*, an *eight*, not a *seven*, when we spoke of a week. We
meant a seven-day-week, although we said eight days.

To go back to the original text, you will notice that the Bible
does not say that Jesus was in the heart of the earth for three
days and three nights. It says that *as* Jonah was in the belly
of the whale for three days and nights, *so* Jesus.... If we were
told in the prophecy of Jonah that he was actually in the fish
for three consecutive periods of twenty-four hours, then we
would have to change our dating of the story of the crucifixion
and resurrection. Jonah, apparently, was in the whale for some
thirty-six hours: the account of the death and resurrection
throws light on the story of Jonah at this point.

But why can we be so sure about the dating of the events
of the death and resurrection of Christ? The answer appears
to me to lie in the Bible teaching about the new creation.

The resurrection of Jesus began a new creation. It was
Genesis chapter 1 all over again. But this time it is a new *spiritual*
creation. Notice the sequence: on the sixth day, Friday, the
sixth day when in the first creation Adam was created, the last
Adam laid down his life. On the Saturday, when in the first
creation God rested, ceased from all his labours, Jesus also
rested. And then on the first day of the week, the day when

in the first creation the actual process of creation began, Jesus rose from the dead to begin a new creation:

> Therefore, if any one is in Christ, he is a new creation; the old has passed away, behold, the new has come (2 Corinthians 5:17).

Why does the creed say that Jesus 'descended into hell'?

We have already seen that the Bible does not teach the idea of death as unconsciousness, or as 'sleep'. But we have also seen that following the creation pattern Jesus died on the sixth day, 'rested' on the seventh day and rose from the dead on the first day. But while Jesus' *body* remained in the grave on the sabbath day, the day of resting, Jesus, the Son of God, the second person of the Trinity, was not asleep. He was not unconscious and he was not in the tomb. We are not told very much about where he was, or what he was doing, but Peter tells us that Jesus went and preached to the spirits 'in prison' (1 Peter 3:19).

Actually we need to look more carefully at the passage in 1 Peter if we are to understand this verse. Verse 18 tells us that Christ died for sins, in order to bring us to God. That's clear enough. Then Peter continues, '... being put to death in the flesh but made alive in the spirit,' and that's clear enough too. He died physically on the cross, but as Paul put it, Jesus became the first fruits of the dead; he was alive in the spirit. Now let's paraphrase the next part:

> And it was in the spirit that Jesus went and made proclamation to the spirits in prison. These spirits refused to believe or obey God long ago, actually while Noah was still building the ark (the ark which meant salvation for just a handful of eight people) (1 Peter 3:18–20).

I think that it is reasonable to join this particular passage with another written by Peter, but in his second letter:

> For if God did not spare the angels [the Greek word just means *messengers*] when they sinned, but cast them into hell [*Tartarus*

seems to be used here to distinguish this place from *Sheol*, since it is spiritual beings, not human beings, who are kept here] and committed them to pits of nether gloom to be kept until the judgement; ... then the Lord knows how to rescue the godly (2 Peter 2:4–9).

I say that it seems reasonable to connect these two passages, partly because they deal with the same fallen and imprisoned spirits, and partly because the period of time referred to is the same in the two passages: 1 Peter 3:20 mentions Noah, and so does 2 Peter 2:5.

Along with these two passages from Peter we may note also Jude's reference to what appears to be the same event:

And the angels that did not keep their own position but left their proper dwelling have been kept by him in eternal chains in the nether gloom until the judgement of the great day (Jude 6).

Exactly what this rebellion was we are not told. The rebellion took place in the days of Noah and so was different from that which led to the original fall of Satan. Since the second spiritual fall was at a time of general world-wide spiritual apostasy when

the Lord saw that the wickedness of man was great in the earth, and that every imagination of the thoughts of his heart was only evil continually (Genesis 6:5)

it is possible that there were spiritual forces allied with man in his revolt against God. At all events God dealt with both acts of rebellion. With the exception of the family of Noah, man was destroyed from the earth, and the angels who had rebelled were imprisoned.

But as with man, so with the spiritual world: sin was not dealt with until Calvary, and the grave and the resurrection. If we dare to express such a possibility, had Satan been able to turn Christ back from the cross, had Christ surrendered to any one of the temptations in the desert, those imprisoned spirits might yet have escaped the ultimate judgement.

But when Christ went to them it was *not* to 'preach' in the sense of offering pardon. The word 'preach' here means 'proclaim'. When Christ descended to Sheol and to Tartarus it was to announce to rebellious man and spirit his own total obedience to his Father, and the certainty of judgement to come. But it was not only that: Jesus proclaimed there the truth that has inspired men and women down the ages, and is surely an immense encouragement to Christians today: over the power of death God has won a certain and inevitable victory.

APPENDIX
LIFE AFTER DEATH IN OTHER RELIGIONS

This question raises a second and very important question: what *is* a religion? It's not too easy to say exactly what we mean by a religion: it's not necessary even for a religion to tell us about God. Buddhism is certainly a religion, but Gautama the Buddha was agnostic about the existence of God. He didn't say too much about the gods.

I would define religion as being any system of thought that tries to provide answers to the ultimate questions. The ultimate questions are 'Where did I come from?', 'Where am I going to?' and 'Why am I here?'. Other ultimate questions concern the world: 'Where did the world come from?', 'Where is the world going to?' and 'Why?'.

On this definition of religion we would include Christianity, Buddhism, Islam, Confucianism, Hinduism, Judaism and communism as religions. They all try to provide answers to the ultimate question. It is very interesting to notice that they do not all give the same answers to the ultimate questions. For example, to the question 'Where did the world come from?', the Christian would answer 'God created it', the Hindu would answer, 'It was not created, it is eternal and yet it is *maya*, a myth.' Communism would answer, 'This world is simply a cosmic accident.'

With the exception of atheistic communism most religions seem to believe in the continuance of life after death. It has, however, been interesting to see new types of communism developing, particularly in Africa, which are not atheistic. So we had a Muslim state like Somalia proclaiming itself communist ... but it was not atheistic communism that the

Somalis accepted, because Islam does believe in life after death. The Muslim belief is, in fact, a mixture of Jewish, Christian and Zoroastrian beliefs about life after death. For the Muslim there are seven heavens and there are seven hells. Some Muslims believe that no Muslim ever goes to hell, but others believe that most Muslims do, and remain there in the seventh hell, the top one, until their sins are paid for or until a Prophet intercedes for them, when they pass to Paradise.

Buddhists and Hindus have a mixture of beliefs, usually involving some form of re-incarnation. This belief sees man as for ever involved with the struggle to opt out of life, to escape from the wheel of existence in this world. Re-incarnation may be in the form of an animal, even of a gnat, or a spider. Where someone has lived a good life, where the desire for things, and especially the desire for personal existence, has been conquered, re-incarnation may be as a priest. Eventually you may hope to escape from this cycle of rebirth and enter into *nirvana* (or *nibbana*) which is not extinction, nor is it a continuing personal existence, but a kind of absorption into the ultimate . . . whatever that might mean. Actually this doctrine has proved rather unacceptable to many Buddhists, and alternative schemes have developed, sometimes involving entry into a Paradise very like the Christian heaven.

It is certainly interesting to study the world's traditional religions, all of which seem to take it for granted that death is a gateway into another existence, not the end of life. Very often arrangements are made to ensure that when a body is buried it is accompanied by tools or money to be used in the next life. Amongst the Egyptians there was even the practice of killing a Pharaoh's servants, and burying them with him when he died, so that they could continue to serve him in the afterlife.

Basically, therefore, all religions seem to believe in life after death, except atheistic communism. But with the wholesale massacres which have accompanied communistic revolutions in Russia and China, and more recently in Cambodia, one can understand why the leaders of communism would not want any afterlife!

FURTHER READING

Bane, Kutscher, Neale & Reeves (ed.), *Death and Ministry* (Seabury Press, 1975).

Joseph Bayly, *The Last Thing We Talk About* (Scripture Union, 1970).

Elizabeth Kubler Ross, *On Death and Dying* (Tavistock Publications, 1970).

Weldon & Levitt, *Is There Life After Death?* (Kingsway Publications, 1978).

C. S. Lewis, *A Grief Observed* (Faber & Faber, 1961).

Basilea Schlink, *What Comes After Death?* (Lakeland, 1976).

Paul Tournier, *Learning to Grow Old* (SCM Press, 1972).

INDEX